A WHOLE NEW BALL GAME

A Whole New

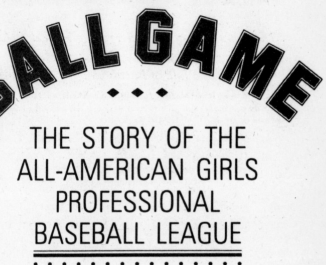

BALL GAME

... · ·

THE STORY OF THE
ALL-AMERICAN GIRLS
PROFESSIONAL
BASEBALL LEAGUE

· · · · · · · · · · · ·

by Sue Macy

PUFFIN BOOKS

PUFFIN BOOKS

Published by the Penguin Group

Penguin Books USA Inc., 375 Hudson Street, New York, New York 10014, U.S.A.

Penguin Books Ltd, 27 Wrights Lane, London W8 5TZ, England

Penguin Books Australia Ltd, Ringwood, Victoria, Australia

Penguin Books Canada Ltd, 10 Alcorn Avenue, Toronto, Ontario, Canada M4V 3B2

Penguin Books (N.Z.) Ltd, 182-190 Wairau Road, Auckland 10, New Zealand

Penguin Books Ltd, Registered Offices: Harmondsworth, Middlesex, England

First published in the United States of America by Henry Holt and Company, Inc., 1993
Reprinted by arrangement with Henry Holt and Company, Inc.
Published in Puffin Books, 1995

1 3 5 7 9 10 8 6 4 2

Library of Congress Cataloging-in-Publication Data
Macy, Sue.
A whole new ball game : the story of the All-American Girls
Professional Baseball League / by Sue Macy.
p.   cm.
Originally published: New York : H. Holt, 1993.
ISBN 0-14-037423-X
1. All-American Girls Professional Baseball League—History—Juvenile literature.
2. Baseball—United States—History—20th century—Juvenile literature.
3. Women baseball players—United States—Juvenile literature.
[GV875.A56M33 1995]   796.357'64'0973—dc20   94-46789   CIP
AC

"All-American Babe," by Phil Stack, *Esquire*, September 1944.
Reprinted with the permission of *Esquire* magazine and the Hearst Corporation.

"Annabelle Lee Again Arouses Poet's Muse," by K. C. Clapp, *Grand Rapids Herald*, July 10, 1945.
Reprinted with the permission of the *Grand Rapids Herald*.

Printed in the United States of America

To the Women
of the AAGPBL

Even today, when spring comes around, I think, "Gosh, years ago I'd be getting ready to go to spring training." The smell of the earth coming alive again, it just brings back memories that make you want to go get out your baseball mitt.

Shirley Stovroff,
South Bend Blue Sox,
1948–1952

Contents

Acknowledgments

Amelia Earhart was my hero when I was growing up. It's not so much that I wanted to be a pilot. It's just that her courage, her determination to do what others thought women couldn't do, inspired me to believe that I could soar to any heights. Had I known about the All-American Girls Professional Baseball League, Jean Faut, Audrey Wagner, Faye Dancer, and their teammates would have laid equal claim to my imagination. Like Earhart, they also dared to defy tradition and live out their dreams.

It is the women of the league who ultimately are responsible for this book, for they refused to let history forget them. By publishing newsletters, organizing reunions, and lobbying for inclusion in the National Baseball Hall of Fame, they kept the spirit of the AAGPBL alive until the world was ready to rediscover it. Their persistence was infectious. It motivated me to continue my work on the league despite jobs and other distractions.

While the ball players were pioneers in sports, Merrie Fidler was a pioneer in sports history. Fidler's 1976 masters thesis was the only available manuscript on the league when I started my own research. I greatly appreciate her generosity in sharing that work with me. I am grateful as well to Sharon Roepke, the undisputed authority on league statistics. She helped me fill in some missing numbers and graciously granted me permission to reprint the AAGBL baseball cards in Chapter 5. My thanks also go to Diane Barts and her staff at the Northern Indiana Historical Society, for photo research above and beyond the call of duty.

In addition, I would like to express my appreciation to the following people for their help along the way:

To Estelle Freedman, who first taught me to seek lessons from women of the past;

To Abby Jungreis, June English, and Julie Winterbottom, for their moral and critical support, and their friendship;

To my colleagues at Scholastic Inc., especially Carol Drisko, for training me to be a professional writer, and Ernie Fleishman, for allowing me the time to finish this book;

To my editor, Marc Aronson, for continually challenging me to do better;

To my cats, Mickey and Lacey, for keeping me company as I wrote by contentedly napping on my desk—and on my source material;

To my father, for teaching me to love baseball; my brother, for respecting me as a sister and a ball player; and my mother, for always having confidence in my ability to write;

And to Sheila Wolinsky, for her unending support and patience as I struggled to find just the right words to tell this story.

Notes on Names

Throughout this book, players are referred to by the names they used during their years in the league. If a woman was married and played under her married name, that's how she appears (for example, Olive Bend Little). If she was married but continued to use her maiden name in the official records, she appears here under her maiden name (for example, Jean Faut). If she married after leaving the league, she appears in the text under her maiden name.

Also, the league's official name changed many times, from the original All-American Girls Softball League (AAGSBL) in early 1943 to the American Girls Baseball League (AGBL) in 1954. During the 1980s the former players adopted the All-American Girls Professional Baseball League (AAGPBL) as their name of choice. In this book, the original name and initials (AAGSBL) are used when referring to the league before the first name change, in July 1943. After that, the league is referred to as the AAGPBL.

Foreword: Welcome to Cooperstown

What are all these *old women* doing here?"

On November 5, 1988, that was the question of the day in Cooperstown, New York. It seemed that the quaint village, home to the very male National Baseball Hall of Fame, suddenly was overrun with women. They came from California, Arizona, Indiana, even Manitoba and Saskatchewan, Canada. Women called Slats and Beans and Frisco and Tex crowded into the hotels and restaurants, acting more like 20-year-olds than gray-haired retirees. The refined streets of Cooperstown were filled with their bear hugs, backslaps, and hearty cries of "How the hell are you?" No one could blame these women if their enthusiasm got the better of them on this crisp autumn Saturday. Three and a half decades after their accomplishments faded into history, they were about to be honored as sports pioneers.

For 12 years, from 1943 through 1954, the women who now gathered in Cooperstown had played in the first, and only, women's professional baseball league. When America's top male baseball players joined up to serve their country during World War II, Chicago Cubs owner Philip K. Wrigley started to worry. Wrigley wanted to make sure baseball fans on the homefront continued to spend their time, and money, at the ballpark. So he decided to form a professional women's league, which would, he said, "furnish additional means of healthful recreation to the public, who are all in one way or another under severe pressure from war work." As a first step he instructed the Cubs' baseball scouts to find him the most promising female ball players in North America. Implicit in these instructions was the order to search for only white athletes. Although there were outstanding African-American women ball players in the United States, none were invited to try out for the new league. (See Chapter 5 for a discussion of this issue.)

Wrigley hired 64 women to play in his new All-American Girls league in 1943, but eventually more than 550 would wear the uniforms of the AAGPBL. On that November day in 1988, 147 former players made their way to Cooperstown, along with hundreds more friends, family members, and fans. Catcher/outfielder Sarah Jane "Salty" Sands brought her 88-year-old father, who had spent more than 30 years bragging about his daughter's baseball accomplishments. Outfielder Lois "Tommie" Barker brought so many supporters that she had to charter a Greyhound bus to get them there.

Accompanying these baseball women were a few baseball men who in a way owed their own careers to the AAGPBL. Major leaguer Casey Candaele learned the tricks of his trade from his mother, outfielder Helen Callaghan. And former major league pitcher Bill "Spaceman" Lee says he got his competitive nature, and some valuable pitching lessons, from his aunt, hurler Annabelle "Lefty" Lee.

At one P.M. on November 5, Candaele and Lee were part of

◆ "Women in Baseball" display at the National Baseball Hall of Fame. AAGPBL lifetime roster is at bottom right. *National Baseball Library, Cooperstown, N.Y.*

the crowd that made its way through the arched doorways of the Hall of Fame Museum, where bronze plaques honor Babe Ruth, Hank Aaron, Willie Mays, and other American heroes. They filed upstairs past the exhibit on the old Negro leagues and stopped at a covered display case across the room. A few moments later a cheer erupted as the cloth was lifted from the case to reveal "Women in Baseball," the first collection in the Hall of Fame to acknowledge women's contributions to the national pastime.

"Women in Baseball" includes photographs of women umpires and women who owned major league teams, but the display centers on the All-American Girls Professional Baseball League. There are AAGPBL balls, bats, uniforms, and yearbooks. There are also photographs of such standouts as first baseman Dorothy Kamenshek, who many feel was the league's best all-around player, and center fielder Faye

Dancer, whose baseball talent was matched only by her flashy, crowd-pleasing style. In the right-hand corner of the exhibit, though, is something that gives every AAGPBL player the right to say she's made it into the Hall of Fame. There, a lifetime roster lists each player along with her hometown and the years that she played in the league.

A few weeks after that autumn day in Cooperstown, June Peppas, president of the AAGPBL Players' Association, sat in her Michigan home writing a letter to the former players. "If we never do any more," Peppas wrote, "we have gotten our display there for all of America to see. Every man, woman, boy, and especially girl that travels through those hallowed halls will now see the All-American Girls Professional Baseball League. For this we should all be very, very proud."

A Whole New Ball Game tells the story of the proud women who played in the AAGPBL. It is a story of life on the homefront during World War II, and of women's changing "place" in society at that time in history. But it is also a story of baseball. For the women of the All-American Girls Professional Baseball League were every bit as in love with the game as the men who made it to the majors. They left their families, their friends, and often their jobs for the chance to play big-time ball.

"My dad managed the men's team in my town," remembered Canadian Velma Abbott, "and I caught batting practice for them. I always dreamed of playing professional baseball. When I was in high school, I saw a magazine article on the league, and I vowed that I'd play in it. It turned out to be one of the greatest experiences a gal could ever have."

◆ Cover of a souvenir program from an AAGPBL rookie touring team game, 1949. *Courtesy of Fran Janssen*

CHAPTER
1

War, Women, and Pro Baseball

World War II started when I was a senior in high school," All-Star pitcher Jean Faut remembered years later, "and everything else seemed to stop. There was no gas for driving a car, except to go to work. Our senior trip became nonexistent. My sister and I were scheduled to go to the Olympics, but they were also canceled. Every boy in my class enlisted. They didn't wait to be drafted. They went." With life suddenly gone haywire, Americans on the homefront took comfort in whatever diversions they could find. Faut's choice was baseball. "Baseball was very important to me," she said. "I lived in a small town, and the only thing left to do was play baseball. There was a men's semipro team which practiced every evening close to my home. I used to pitch batting practice for them."

When the war was over, Faut displayed her skills as perhaps the best overhand pitcher in the All-American Girls Professional Baseball League. She owed her baseball career to the very changes that had thrown her life into confusion.

Ironically, the tragic events that were played out in Europe, Africa, and Asia during the war gave Faut and 550 other women the chance to realize their dreams.

Female baseball players were not the only women to find extraordinary opportunities during the war. Against a backdrop of catastrophe, American women rose to a wide variety of new challenges. This liberating experience added another chapter to the ever-changing story of women's role in American life. It came on the heels of a decade when women took a step backward in social and economic progress. In the 1930s, the United States suffered through a devastating economic depression. At its height in 1933, nearly 13 million people— one out of every four American workers—were unemployed. Women, especially married women, bore the largest share of the burden. To help get male workers back on their feet, national leaders called for married women in two-income families to give up their jobs. As a result, eight states barred married women from holding state jobs. Three out of every four American cities barred married women from teaching school. And 26 of the 48 states introduced bills barring married women from all paying jobs. (Only one state, Louisiana, passed such a law. It was quickly declared unconstitutional.)

After the United States entered World War II in December 1941, attitudes toward women workers changed virtually overnight. By the summer of 1943, 10 million men had joined or been drafted into the U.S. armed forces. The sudden rush to go to war left scores of homefront businesses understaffed. Restaurants that had previously depended on male waiters switched to cafeteria service. Hotel bellboys were no longer "boys," but men who were too old to join the military. Plumbers, doctors, and auto mechanics increasingly became hard to find.

The United States was suffering from a "manpower" shortage when it needed workers most. America's fighting forces

U. S. ARMY
OFFICIAL POSTER

SOLDIERS *without guns*

◆ One in a series of posters issued by the government to encourage women to join the war effort. *Library of Congress*

had to have guns, tanks, ships, and planes, but the factories that could produce them had lost many of their employees to the military. Who could fill the jobs in these vital wartime industries? The government turned to the previously under-valued portions of the work force: women and minorities. "In some communities employers dislike to hire women," President Franklin D. Roosevelt said in an October 1942 speech. "In others they are reluctant to hire Negroes. We can no longer afford to indulge such prejudice."

Soon after Roosevelt's speech, the government began an ambitious campaign to convince women to do their patriotic duty and "man" the nation's factories. "Do the Job *HE* Left Behind," urged one poster. "If you've sewed on buttons," a billboard declared, "you can learn to weld on airplane parts." The campaign succeeded. Attracted by the good pay of factory jobs, as well as by the chance to help their country, more than 6 million women joined the work force for the first time during the war.

As women headed for the factories, a new wartime heroine was born. "Rosie the Riveter" was the subject of songs, films, magazine covers, and posters. This mythical war worker glorified a job held by many women in airplane factories. Riveters worked in teams to help build planes. One riveter shot a rivet, or metal pin, into the metal plates that formed the plane, and the other riveter flattened the pin in place. The work took a lot of muscle, and Rosie the Riveter was portrayed as strong, tough, and attractive, a new image for women.

In the fall of 1942, Rosie the Riveter was very much on Philip K. Wrigley's mind. President of the William Wrigley Jr. chewing-gum company, Wrigley was also the owner of the Chicago Cubs National League baseball team. And he was worried about what the war was doing to baseball. The major leagues had already lost more than half of their players to the military, replacing them with men who were too old to be drafted and boys who were too young. The minor leagues, where younger players got experience for the majors, were

◆ Two "Rosie the Riveters." During World War II, 19 percent of African-American women worked "on the line" in factories, up from 7 percent before the war. *Library of Congress*

even harder hit. By the start of the 1943 season, more than 3,000 minor leaguers had joined the service or taken war-related jobs on the homefront. Only nine of the nation's 26 minor leagues had enough men left to play ball.

Despite the life-and-death struggles going on overseas, baseball was a topic that got its own share of national attention. On January 16, 1942, President Roosevelt wrote a letter to the Commissioner of Baseball, Judge Kenesaw Mountain Landis, urging that major league ball continue. "I honestly feel that it would be best for the country to keep baseball going," wrote Roosevelt. "There will be fewer people unemployed and everybody will work longer hours and harder than ever before. And that means they ought to have a chance for recreation and for taking their minds off their work. . . . Even if the actual quality of the teams is lowered by the greater use of older players, this will not dampen the popularity of the sport."

Philip Wrigley never doubted that sports could play an important role in keeping up morale on the homefront. But if Roosevelt changed his mind, Wrigley wanted to be ready with a backup plan. In the fall of 1942, he assigned a three-man team from the Cubs organization to look into the possibility of developing a professional baseball league with female players. If Rosie the Riveter could keep wartime factories going, maybe Rosie the Right Fielder could do the same for baseball parks.

Although American women had been playing baseball on college and local teams since the 1860s, Wrigley's plan was to start a professional women's *softball* league. Softball had developed in the 1880s as a version of baseball that could be played indoors. The idea was to use a larger, softer ball, which would be difficult to hit long distances. At the time, women's sports experts welcomed the new game. Besides the softer ball, indoor baseball called for lighter bats and shorter base paths. That seemed to promise fewer injuries and greater success for girls.

Interest in indoor baseball eventually died out, but the use of the larger ball and the smaller playing field caught on. In the 1910s and '20s, recreation groups moved indoor baseball outdoors, setting up leagues that held their games on play-grounds. "Playground ball," or "softball," got another big boost during the Depression, when unemployed Americans started playing the game in parks and on vacant lots. In 1933 Chicago's Century of Progress World's Fair sponsored the first national softball championships for men and women. Four years later, a survey found that 12 million Americans played softball. By 1943 *Time* magazine estimated that there were some 40,000 semipro women's softball teams in the United States.

While women's softball was growing in popularity during the 1930s, female athletes were gaining star status in other, individual sports. Philip Wrigley had no doubt that the top women softball players could become just as famous. "In two or three years' time it's possible that girls' softball may be recognized by the press and radio as of major league possi-bilities," he wrote in February 1943. "When that time arrives, girl [softball players] will have the same opportunity to gain nationwide recognition and acclaim as . . . Helen Wills and Helen Jacobs in Tennis; Patty Berg and Helen Hicks in Golf; Gertrude Ederle, Gloria Callen, and Eleanor Holm in Swim-ming."

By January 1943, Wrigley's committee had brought back optimistic reports on the appeal of a women's professional softball league in the United States. The following month, Wrigley met with the owners of the seven other National League baseball teams. He presented the plan for his All-American Girls Softball League and asked if the owners would let the women play in their stadiums when the men's teams were on the road. The owners said no. They felt that baseball fans in their cities didn't have the time or money to go to both men's and women's games.

Branch Rickey of the Brooklyn Dodgers didn't offer his

team's ballpark, but he did think a women's league was a good idea. Like Philip Wrigley, Rickey was a baseball pioneer. He was the first major league official to hire players from Cuba, and in 1945 he signed Jackie Robinson, the first African-American man to play in the majors in the twentieth century. Rickey didn't become involved in the day-to-day activities of Wrigley's league, but he did become a trustee, or director. His support helped give the All-American Girls league its reputation as a first-class operation.

Without the use of the National League stadiums, the women's teams couldn't play in the nation's largest metropolitan areas. So Wrigley turned to medium-sized cities closer to home. The league's first four teams were located in South Bend, Indiana; Rockford, Illinois; and Kenosha and Racine, Wisconsin. All four cities were industrial centers within a hundred miles of Chicago, full of men and women who were busy building tanks and weapons in factories that used to produce cars and lawn mowers. These workers were at the heart of the homefront war effort. Wrigley figured his women's league would be just the thing to help them relax after a hard day on the assembly line.

While Wrigley worked out the business details of the league, 30 of his baseball scouts searched the United States and Canada for top women ball players. Although the four teams had room for a total of only 64 players, hundreds of women showed up for the initial tryouts, held in a dozen major cities. In May 1943 some 280 of them were invited to Wrigley Field in Chicago for the final selection process. They came from 26 states and five Canadian provinces.

In Chicago league officials put the players through a series of tests. "You played your position, you ran, you slid, you did everything," remembered Dorothy Kamenshek, one of the league's first and most successful players. "They started

◆ The first four players signed for the AAGSBL. Sitting: Shirley Jameson. Standing, left to right: Clara Schillace, Ann Harnett, Edie Perlick. *From the Collection of the Northern Indiana Historical Society*

weeding people out almost the first day. You'd be afraid to answer the phone in your hotel room."

Those who made the cut were in for a challenging summer. Teams in the All-American Girls Softball League played every day and twice on Sundays, for a total of 108 games each in 1943. And these longtime softball players had to learn to play by new rules. Softball teams usually had ten players on the field, but Wrigley's teams used only nine. Base runners were allowed to lead off and steal bases. And the pitcher stood 40 feet from the batter instead of 35. These were the first in a series of changes that made the league's game faster and more like baseball. As an indication of the changes still to come, Wrigley renamed the league in the middle of its first season. Its new name: the All-American Girls *Baseball* League.

Despite the new rules and the grueling schedule, women jumped at the call to join the league. "It was a chance to get paid for something I would have done for free," said catcher Irene "Tuffy" Hickson. "My mother needed my help at home, but she knew how much I loved to play ball and gave me her blessing. I sent as much money home as I could." With a starting salary of $40 to $85 plus expenses per week, the pay actually was better than women could make in most jobs. "At that time I was teaching," remembered Shirley Jameson, the second woman to sign up. "And my summer salary was more than I made teaching nine months a year!"

Playing in the All-American Girls league was meant to be a total experience. The women were paid relatively well because playing ball was to be their only job during the summer months. Wrigley wanted his players to focus all of their energy on the league. According to a February 1943 letter, he also wanted them "to raise the level of the present game of girls softball." Taking his cue from Rosie the Riveter, Wrigley looked for players who were skilled, strong, and *attractive*. "The All-American Girls Softball League is created with the highest ideals of womanhood in mind," the letter said. An All-American Girl could play like a man, but her fans would never be allowed to forget that she was a woman.

The All-Important
Femininity Angle

When Philip Wrigley started the All-American Girls Softball League in 1943, he was well aware of the public's image of women softball players. And he didn't like it a bit. "The frailest creature on the diamond is frequently the male umpire," reported an article on women's softball in the August 22, 1942, issue of the *Saturday Evening Post*. The article included a photograph of a woman player spitting a perfect stream of water through her teeth. "Give 'em a cud of tobacco," it went on to say, "and these female softball players would look just like their big-league brothers—almost."

Wrigley's staff, including his advertising director Arthur E. Meyerhoff, set out to combat this image from the start. In a letter sent to potential players in 1943, they wrote, "Our research work has proven beyond a doubt that the game, as now played, has taken a definite step toward aping the game of baseball—a man's game. The game as played by the All-American Girls Softball League will be truly a feminine game without taking away any of the thrilling action. . . . The natural appeal of women in every walk of life will be brought out in this venture. Girls will dress, act and carry themselves as befits the feminine sex."

Indeed, Wrigley and his staff were determined to ensure the AAGSBL's success by carefully controlling almost every aspect of their players' appearance and behavior. Their efforts started with the players' uniforms. At the time, most women played softball wearing satin shirts with shorts or baseball pants. Wrigley charged his uniform committee, including his wife Helen, artist Otis Shepherd, and Chicago softball star Ann Harnett, with the task of designing an outfit that was more "feminine."

The committee's final design was inspired by the field hockey and figure skating outfits of the day. Ball players would wear a one-piece dress with a three-quarter-length flared skirt and satin briefs underneath. These uniforms were praised as "dainty, pastel frocks" by the *Rockford* (Illinois) *Register-Republican*, but the players found them less than practical. Pitchers had to pin their skirts down to avoid hitting them when they took their windmill windups, and base runners collected huge assortments of bruises and "strawberries" from sliding with bare legs.

Even though the uniforms made it necessary for base runners to be extra tough, Wrigley directed his All-American Girls to be poised and "feminine" at all times. He was selling a wholesome product to Midwestern fans, and he wanted to make sure the competitive spirits of his players never interfered with their ladylike image. It was an impossible expectation. "Most of us thought it was a big joke," remembered Dorothy Kamenshek. "I mean, how were we supposed to develop this real slinky walk when we were playing baseball?" But Wrigley anticipated players' objections and offered them help in meeting the challenge. At spring training, after

◆ Spring training, 1944—A Ruth Tiffany instructor (in hat) shows her All-American students how to sit "like ladies." Pitcher Carolyn Morris, a model in the off-season, is at far right. *Courtesy of Connie Wisniewski*

days filled with batting practice and fielding drills, the women went to night school to work on their "charm."

Run by the Helena Rubinstein Salon in 1943 and the Ruth Tiffany School in 1944, the league's nighttime charm school included lessons in the arts of walking, sitting, speaking, selecting clothes, applying makeup, and other everyday activities. According to the Ruth Tiffany School, these lessons were meant to help each player become "a *bright* star, casting her radiance in many circles." A handbook given out to the players reminded them that "your mind and your body are interrelated and you cannot neglect one without causing the other to suffer. A healthy mind and a healthy body are the true attributes of the All-American girl." The handbook also recommended the cosmetics each player should have in her

"All-American Girls Baseball League Beauty Kit," including cleansing cream, lipstick, rouge, deodorant, a mild astringent, face powder, hand lotion, and hair remover.

Among the players, charm school provoked a wide range of reactions, from appreciation to disbelief. "It made an impression on me," said center fielder Thelma "Tiby" Eisen. "I think that a lot of the girls needed it. They had no polish. I always felt that if you were going to be in the public eye, you might as well have a little class." Yet a number of players admit to skipping charm school when they could. "Once I snuck out with two other players down the fire escape," remembered left fielder Jo Lenard. "And when the lady who was teaching the course saw me the next day, she said, 'Gee, I didn't see you there, Jo. You really missed something because the league spent about a thousand dollars to get this course.' I said, 'Honey, they could spend ten thousand. It wouldn't change me one bit.'"

Some players resented the fact that the emphasis on social behavior took the spotlight away from their athletic accomplishments. Indeed, a number of male sportswriters, who were skeptical about the women's league to begin with, filed sarcastic reports about "powder puff baseball" and the "carefully coiffured cuties" who played it. "'Quick, Millie, my mask and my mascara,'" began an article by the United Press in May 1944. "There's a powder puff plot under way at 3 P.M. Saturday at Nicollet Park which threatens the foundation of the national pastime, a conspiracy aimed at virtual extinction of the perspiring, swearing, tobacco-chewing baseball player."

Although this and similar articles made some of the women bristle, they fit neatly into Philip Wrigley's plans. Wrigley was more concerned with transforming the behavior of women athletes than with challenging ideas about women's role in

◆ Annabelle Lee (left) and Alma Ziegler get lessons in diction from a charm school instructor, 1944. *From the Collection of the Northern Indiana Historical Society*

society. Whenever possible, he and advertising director Meyerhoff helped writers point out how their players exemplified the "feminine" ideal. Meyerhoff provided the press with background information on the most glamorous players, and the resulting articles often focused on the women's personal lives. A feature on pitcher Carolyn Morris showed her modeling scarves at her winter job at a Chicago women's store. An article on shortstop Dottie Schroeder included a picture of her stepping out of the shower and reported that "Dottie and her teammates live sort of a double life. They do their work like men and dream of living like all women do, after the ball game ends."

◆ Pitcher Beverly Hatzell applies lipstick with the help of her catcher, Anna Mae O'Dowd, 1949. Posed photos often showed players checking their makeup during games. *Courtesy of Sophie Kurys*

It was important to Philip Wrigley that the public see his league as an institution in which femininity and ball-playing skill went hand in hand. Wrigley even hired a female chaperone for each team. Described as "a combination housemother, first-aid specialist, Emily Post, and cop on the beat," the chaperone was the team's off-the-field manager, responsible for everything from bandaging bruises to approving players' living quarters. But she also was Wrigley's moral watchdog, there to make sure that the players lived up to their upstanding image. It was the chaperone's duty to see that the women followed the rules that outlined how they should act in public.

Not surprisingly, these player conduct rules emphasized femininity and healthy competition. From the start, the rules included the following:

1. Always appear in feminine attire when not actively engaged in practice or playing ball. At no time may a player appear in the stands in her uniform.

2. Smoking and drinking are not permitted in public places.

3. All social engagements must be approved by the chaperones.

4. All living quarters and eating places must be approved by the chaperones.

5. [On road trips] each club will establish a satisfactory place to eat and a time when all members must be in their individual rooms. In general, the lapse of time will be two hours after the finish of the last game.

6. In order to sustain the complete spirit of rivalry between clubs, the members of the different clubs must not fraternize [socialize] at any time during the season.

To Wrigley, these and the other conduct rules served two purposes. First, they set a standard of behavior his players had to live up to. And second, they helped to show the public that the All-American Girls league was a well-disciplined, honorable organization. The rules, and the presence of chaperones to carry them out, had the added benefit of winning over the parents of would-be players. Betty "Moe" Trezza was just 18 when she left her home in Brooklyn, New York, to join the league's Minneapolis Millerettes. The "baby" in a family of 12 children, Trezza remembered, "My mother wouldn't let me play until I convinced her we'd be chaperoned."

The All-American Girls league continued to emphasize the conduct rules, with some changes, throughout its 12-year history. And although there were no charm school classes after 1944, players periodically were reminded of the importance of being "feminine." In March 1950, Racine Belles president Don Black sent his players a six-page letter to prepare them for the coming season. "Our league and our club have only two important things to sell the public," Black wrote, "playing ability and femininity. While the playing ability of our teams has been steadily on the increase, we must not forget and grow lax about the all-important femininity angle. It was one of the prime factors on which our league was founded and it is more than ever important that it should remain.

"You'd be surprised at the importance this holds with the average fan," Black continued. "Nobody is especially surprised or impressed if a rough, tough mannish looking babe shows some ability at sports. But to realize that a truly feminine creature can reach the top in one branch of athletic endeavor is refreshing and pleasing. Your fans want you to look and act like ladies and still play ball like gentlemen!"

While the rules on feminine dress and behavior were enforced right through 1954, other rules were sometimes ignored. Pitcher Fran Janssen remembered driving to visit players in Kalamazoo, Michigan, when her own games in Fort Wayne were rained out. That clearly broke the rule about not socializing with players on other teams, but Janssen never got into trouble for it. "The rules were there," said Janssen, "but I think people ignored them more. Of course, the players got older too, and that probably made a little difference."

In the 1950s the league made a change that weakened the role of the team chaperone. To save money, the board of directors voted to allow teams to have a player double as a chaperone. "It was very rough to try to do those two things at once," said catcher Shirley Stovroff, who was the player-chaperone for the 1952 South Bend Blue Sox. "One evening

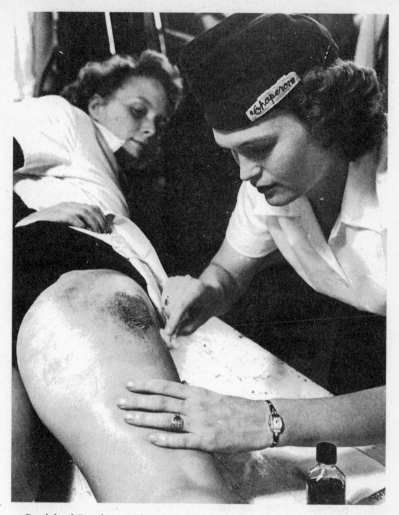

◆ Rockford Peaches pitcher Lois Florreich pays the price for sliding in a skirt. Player/chaperone Dottie Green tends to her strawberry. *National Baseball Library, Cooperstown, N.Y.*

Dottie Mueller, one of our pitchers, broke a couple of fingers in a fight. She had swung at someone and hit the wall instead." Stovroff knew what had happened, but she didn't want to jeopardize Mueller's standing with the Blue Sox. "I told Karl Winsch, the manager, that Dottie had gotten out of a cab and slammed the door on her hand," she remembered.

Despite her own frustrations as a chaperone, Shirley Stovroff understood the league's emphasis on discipline and femininity. "Actually I think it was a good thing," she said. "We're talking about the 1940s and 1950s. If they had come out and allowed the women to do whatever they wanted to and wear whatever they wanted to, it would have gone against the grain of the conservative people." Like Stovroff, many players and officials ultimately valued the league's rules and restrictions and cited them as important ingredients in the league's success. Since the All-American Girls behaved the way society expected them to off the field, they earned the public's respect, and often their admiration, as ball players. In the world of the 1940s and '50s, conforming to public expectations was the surest way for Wrigley's league to gain acceptance.

Although times have changed since Wrigley's day, more recent experiments in women's sports have reflected his strategy. In 1979 and 1980, the California Dreams of the short-lived Women's Professional Basketball League (WBL) sent their players to charm school. Another WBL team, the New Orleans Pride, hired a makeup specialist to help players apply cosmetics before each home game. Even well-established women's sports organizations have highlighted players' sex appeal in an attempt to attract new fans. In the 1980s both the Ladies Professional Golf Association (LPGA) and the Women's Tennis Association (WTA) issued calendars featuring sexy photos of female athletes.

Like basketball players in the WBL, the All-American Girls players put up with their league's "femininity angle" because, more than anything, they wanted to play ball. Long before Philip Wrigley had the brainstorm to start a "girls' league," they had come to love the sights, the sounds, the smells of the baseball diamond. Wrigley's league offered these women keen competition, decent pay, and the chance to be proud of their athletic talent. If they had to walk around with bruised legs and rouged cheeks, it was a small price to pay.

CHAPTER

Learning the Game

One summer evening in 1944, Rockford Peaches pitcher Carolyn Morris stopped on her way to the ballpark to watch some boys playing sandlot baseball. After a few minutes, Morris asked the boys if she could take a turn at the plate. They handed her a bat, threw her a pitch, and watched, dumbfounded, as she walloped the ball past the farthest outfielder. Returning the bat, the dark-haired 18-year-old flashed a smile at the dazed youngsters. Finally one of them closed his gaping mouth long enough to ask, "Say, lady, have you got a brother who'd like to play ball with us?"

Morris's young admirers weren't the only ones who just didn't know what to make of the women in the AAGPBL. Coming face to face with ball players who hit like Ted Williams but looked like Scarlett O'Hara was enough to throw tradition-bound baseball fans into confusion. Before Wrigley's league, few people were aware of organized competition for women in baseball, and top-level female players were rare. Prevailing attitudes that branded women as "mannish" if they played a "man's" sport kept many girls from competing seriously. Those women who did develop their

◆ Pitcher Carolyn Morris. *From the Collection of the Northern Indiana Historical Society*

baseball skills usually started playing under the guidance of fathers, brothers, or male friends. This early encouragement, plus a growing love of the game, motivated them to continue playing as long as they could resist being redirected into more "feminine" pursuits.

Women who were serious about baseball approached the game with a combination of inspiration, dedication, and a lot of hard work. Pitcher Olive Bend Little got a taste of the hard work early. Little grew up in Poplar Point, Manitoba, Canada, with a hockey-playing brother who made it all the way to the National Hockey League. "My father felt that if you had talent, it was almost a sin to give it less than your best," said Little, who went on to pitch the first no-hitter in the AAGPBL. "From the time I was ten, we spent an hour every night practicing—half an hour fielding ground balls and half an hour pitching. If my father couldn't be there, my two brothers were elected, and sometimes they weren't very happy about that. I can remember one of their dates waiting impatiently as they hit one ball after another to me."

Kay "Swish" Blumetta also started playing ball early, but she was motivated by her love of the game rather than her father's resolve. "I was an only child, but I always cared about sports," remembered the New Jersey-born pitcher, who spent 11 years in the AAGPBL. "I played softball on the playground teams with the boys, and when I got older, I played hardball with the boys. I'd be up at the playground six days a week—it was closed on Sundays. I was the only girl, because I was the tomboy of the neighborhood."

Blumetta was inspired by baseball's competitive spirit—the chance to test her limits, to battle opponents, to be part of a team. Playing ball offered Lavonne "Pepper" Paire all of that, and more. When Paire was nine, she joined a softball team sponsored by a local grocery store. Despite her young age, Paire quickly learned that playing ball could put food on the table. "When we won a game, the store owner would give us an empty grocery bag," Paire remembered. "He'd let us fill it up with whatever we wanted—for free. I'd get plenty of meat, and coffee, and some cakes, too. This was during the Depression, and my father never knew what kind of work he was going to get. Often we'd eat for a week on my groceries."

By the time they made it to the AAGPBL, most women had years of training in softball or baseball. Still, the league's rookies often found that they had more to learn. "The first season I pitched in South Bend, a pop fly went up by the mound," remembered pitcher Ruth Williams. "Well, I had played amateur ball, and the pitcher always fielded her own position. So I'm reaching for the ball, and all of a sudden up comes an arm, and an elbow hits me in the face. It was [South Bend catcher Mary "Bonnie"] Baker. And she yells, *'I'll take it!'* Boy oh boy, she cracked me in the jaw. She said, 'Don't you know that the catcher takes all pop flies?' I said, 'I do now.' "

During one of her first games, catcher Ruth "Tex" Lessing got an equally memorable initiation into the pros. Early in 1944, Lessing was behind the plate for the Minneapolis Millerettes as they faced the Milwaukee Chicks and catcher Dorothy "Mickey" Maguire. "Mickey was on third base, and the batter hit a fly ball to left field," remembered Lessing, "and Mickey tried to score after the catch. The left fielder threw the ball to the plate, and Mickey came in sliding, but I had the plate blocked so she was out. Well, she slid into my knee and cut her lip and knocked a couple of teeth loose, and everyone on the bench said, 'She'll get even with you. She doesn't forget.' I wanted to go home right then. Sure enough, later in the game she tried to score from third again after the batter hit a grounder to the shortstop. This time I didn't dare block the plate, but I had the ball and was standing, waiting to tag her. Mickey would have been out by ten feet, but she came barrelling into me. The ball went one way and I went the other, and she was safe. After that, Mickey came back over to me and said, 'Kid, you've got a lot to learn.' "

◆ The runner is safe as catcher Ruth "Tex" Lessing receives a late throw from the infield. *Courtesy of Ruth Lessing*

Like Williams and Lessing, many AAGPBL rookies got memorable lessons in how to play professional ball. While a lot of those lessons came from other players, the women also learned a thing or two from their managers. The 40 or so managers who led AAGPBL teams included six women, Bonnie Baker among them. But the league used women managers only to fill short-term vacancies. The goal of Philip Wrigley and ad man Arthur Meyerhoff was to recruit retired, big-name male athletes who would attract fans. Nearly two thirds of the men who became managers had played baseball in the major or minor leagues.

Perhaps the best known AAGPBL managers were the three

men whose major league accomplishments would land them in the National Baseball Hall of Fame: slugger Jimmy Foxx; base-stealing standout Max Carey; and quick-handed short-stop Dave Bancroft. Of the three, Carey had the greatest impact on the league. After spending 1944 as manager of the Milwaukee Chicks, he became AAGPBL president, oversee-ing the development of the game and setting up a scouting system to find future female stars. Carey continued as presi-dent until 1950, when he returned to managing, this time with the Fort Wayne Daisies. "Max Carey was the best," remembered Tiby Eisen, a base-stealing star in her own right. "He was a great teacher. He brought out the good in every-body."

Not all managers earned the respect that Carey did. Some former players had trouble adjusting to the role of teacher, and a few, including Jimmy Foxx, brought drinking problems with them that ended their AAGPBL careers prematurely. In 1948, the Fort Wayne Daisies came up against a different kind of problem. In a letter to league president Carey, the Daisies Board of Directors explained that "there were nu-merous happenings during the playing season which led us to believe that [first-time manager] Dick Bass was not getting the best results from the girls due to his inexperience in working with the feminine ball players." Among the problems was Bass's "personal relationship" with his second baseman. "Dick Bass was a very nice man," said Tiby Eisen, "but he mixed too many emotions on the team. When you're in love with one of the ball players, it just doesn't go." Fort Wayne dismissed Bass late in the season, and Eisen and two other players managed the remaining games.

If Foxx and Bass were among the league's more problem-atic managers, Bill Allington was among its best. Allington was a smart baseball man and a tough taskmaster with more

◆ The Rockford Peaches in their locker room after a practice session. *From the Collection of the Northern Indiana Historical Society*

than 20 years of experience playing minor league ball. During the AAGPBL's first year, he served as a scout in Los Angeles, where he also coached women's softball and did a bit of movie acting on the side. In 1944, however, Allington headed to the Midwest, bringing along a handful of his softball stars. He stayed with the league until the end, managing the Rockford Peaches for eight years and the Fort Wayne Daisies for two.

Allington's teams topped the league's standings five times and made it to the finals of the postseason play-offs eight out of ten years. His Rockford Peaches took four postseason titles in six years, creating the closest thing to a dynasty that the AAGPBL ever had. What was the key to Allington's success? "Bill was a good teacher," remembered Rockford second baseman Alice Pollit. "We came in as softball players, and he transformed us into baseball players. He knew that we had the ability and he brought it out of us." But Allington was also a strict disciplinarian who regularly put his players through grueling practice drills and spent road trips quizzing them on baseball basics. "Allington was as tough as they came," said Ruth Williams, "but boy, did they play ball for him."

Contemporary newspaper and magazine articles portrayed the AAGPBL's managers as beleaguered and even henpecked by their female players. In 1948 the New York *Sunday News* reported that "one of the first things noticeable about most of the teams is that the managers have white hair. A remark on this usually brings the answer that they had white hair before they came to the league, but if they hadn't, it probably would have turned like that." The following year a writer for *Colliers* magazine repeated a story that he felt illustrated the dilemmas of "the harried men who have to manage" in the league. It seems that Grand Rapids Chicks manager Benny Meyer once had his picture taken with his team, described by the writer as "18 ballet-skirted, bare-thighed, pretty girls." According to *Colliers*, "Several days later, Meyer received a letter from his wife, down home in Arkansas. There was a newspaper clipping of the photograph and, for some reason, Mrs. Meyer had marked Benny with a large X. Benny wired home: 'Dear Ma. It ain't the femininity that gets me. It's the skill.' "

Whenever possible, the AAGPBL used its managers to promote interest in its games, even if that meant making jokes at the players' expense. But a manager's future rested more on his team's success than his ability to charm the press. If a team

◆ White-haired manager Johnny Rawlings instructs his players in the Grand Rapids Chicks dugout, late 1940s. *From the Collection of the Northern Indiana Historical Society*

didn't win ball games, fans would stop coming to the ballpark, and team owners would stop making money. Managers were paid high salaries—sometimes more than $3,600 for the five-month season—to make sure their clubs did well. And when a team had a bad year, it was often the manager who paid the price. Fourteen of the league's 32 male managers held their jobs for one season or less.

The women of the AAGPBL disagreed on the part their managers played in their baseball educations. But whether they learned the most from their managers, their AAGPBL teammates, or their childhood coaches and friends, the result was the same. By overcoming obstacles and following their dreams, the women became athletes to reckon with. Their efforts inspired young girls to plan futures in baseball and old-timers to reevaluate their prejudices against women playing ball. And although Philip Wrigley and his staff carefully developed the images of the league's "feminine" players and harried managers, it was the quality of the women's ball playing that kept fans coming back. "You've got to see those girls play to believe it," an unnamed former manager told *Colliers*. "They slide, steal bases, throw overhand, and pitch curves—and the fans love it."

The War Effort

Women in the All-American Girls Professional Baseball League didn't come much more competitive than Mickey Maguire. The gutsy catcher from Lagrange, Ohio, played her heart out in every game. When Maguire joined the league in 1943, her husband, Corporal Thomas J. Maguire, Jr., was stationed overseas. On June 9, 1944, Maguire took her place behind the plate as usual for her team, the Milwaukee Chicks. Although the Chicks lost to the Kenosha Comets 11–4, the next day's newspapers didn't dwell on the lopsided score. Instead, they reported that the game had featured "the most dramatic exhibition of courage shown in the girls loop in its short, one-season history." Just moments before the first pitch, Maguire received word that her husband had been killed in the fighting in Italy. After making a quiet request that the crowd not be told, she put on her gear, took the field, and played ball.

No one would have blamed Mickey Maguire if she had asked for time off after learning of her husband's death. The fact that she paid tribute to him by digging in her heels and catching a good game says a lot about her determination and

◆ Dorothy "Mickey" Maguire. *National Baseball Library, Coopers-*
town, N.Y.

strength. Her actions also set an example for others who
would face the loss of a loved one during the war. By the end
of the fighting, in August 1945, more than 292,000 American
servicemen had died in battle. Like Maguire, their families
and friends had to carry on the best way they knew how.

While Americans on the homefront worried about the wel-
fare of loved ones overseas, they also faced daily challenges
because of the country's focus on the war. Their lives were
turned upside down by a series of laws passed in 1942 and
1943 to free up food, fuel, and other materials for the mili-

◆ In November 1945, customers at a Seattle, Washington, butcher shop wave their ration books in the air when they learn that meat rationing is about to end. *AP/Wide World Photo*

tary. The laws called for rationing, or limiting the amounts of certain goods that people could buy. By 1943, rationed goods included gasoline, fuel oil, automobile tires, sugar, coffee, butter, meat, baby food, and a number of canned foods, such as peaches, carrots, and milk.

Under rationing, Americans over the age of 16 could apply for books of ration stamps every six months. Each tiny stamp was good for a certain period of time—usually one month—and was worth a certain number of points. To buy rationed goods, a person needed stamps with the required number of points, as well as money to make the actual purchase. If a consumer ran out of stamps for the month, he or she had to wait until the next month to buy more of the rationed goods.

Gasoline rationing in particular had a dramatic effect on the way people lived. Drivers were limited to as little as three gallons of gas per week, barely enough for most people to get to work and do everyday errands. Gas shortages created a captive audience for hometown entertainment, and people flocked to local movie theaters or crowded around living-room radios to escape the pressures of the war. If there was an All-American Girls ball team in town, they also came to games. "All those people needed something to do, to go to," remembered Racine Belles pitcher Joanne Winter. "The people had kids in the war, they had friends in the war. They were worried. So the league was a great contribution."

Philip Wrigley felt that the league's success depended at least partially on its patriotic spirit. Therefore, he often described the creation of the league in terms of the war effort. "The need for additional recreation in towns busy with war defense work prompted the idea for the All-American Girls Softball League," he told the Associated Press in April 1943. Wrigley also dictated that in keeping with a new custom at major league baseball games, each All-American Girls game would begin with "The Star-Spangled Banner." While the music played, the two teams would stand in straight lines that met at home plate, forming a symbolic V for Victory.

Besides providing relaxation and inspiration for war workers, Wrigley made sure the league offered what support it could to the armed services. On July 1, 1943, an All-American Girls All-Star game at Wrigley Field in Chicago doubled as a recruiting drive for the Women's Army Corps, or WAC. The following summer four teams from the league returned to Wrigley Field for a July 18 doubleheader that offered free admission to Red Cross workers, members of the armed forces, and anyone who had donated blood at a Red

◆ Two teams line up in a V for Victory as "The Star-Spangled Banner" plays. *From the Collection of the Northern Indiana Historical Society*

Cross blood drive. The games attracted a crowd of more than 16,000, including matinee idol and guest speaker Victor Mature, but they also were noteworthy for another reason. Until 1988, Wrigley Field had no lights for night games. Special portable lights were set up for the All-American Girls contests, making them the first games ever played after dark at Wrigley Field.

In 1945 the league's commitment to the war effort took an even more ambitious form. That March the league newsletter, *The A-A-G's Mail Bag*, announced the plan. "The second week of spring training is going to be devoted to playing at Army camps in the Sixth Corps area," the *Mail Bag* explained. "That's the news we've been waiting for, and we hope that everything will go along smoothly." The schedule called for the league's six teams to pair up and play games at 13 different army training camps and veterans' hospitals over the course of five days. The tour was so successful that additional exhibition games were scheduled at the end of July.

Spectators at the All-American Girls army-camp games included "battle veterans from the various war sectors, together with untested rookies and battle casualties," according to the *Fort Sheridan* (Illinois) *Tower*. Before and after the games, the players toured hospitals and spoke with wounded soldiers. Fort Wayne Daisies chaperone Helen Rauner Harrington remembered a pregame visit by her team and the Grand Rapids Chicks to the amputees ward at Percy Jones General Hospital. "This is when I found just what those girls were made of," said Harrington. "They went through talking to the guys, asking where they were from and making other small talk, never letting them know any pity. The guys ate it up. At that time we were the same age as those fellows, and many of us had family or friends in the service."

Visiting army camps and hospitals was a natural extension of the personal commitment many players felt to the troops. Several of the women had husbands or brothers fighting overseas, and Rockford Peaches catcher Dottie Green had half a town. In 1944, Green's hometown of Natick, Massachusetts, was cited by the Federal government for having the greatest percentage of servicemen of any town in the United States. Some 1,500 of Natick's 3,000 citizens were serving in the armed forces. In May of that year, Green was honored by the women's division of the Coast Guard for her support of these

◆ Faye Dancer shows the style that made *Life* magazine notice her as she slides to avoid a tag from Marge Wenzel. Dancer claims this is her favorite picture. *From the Collection of the Northern Indiana Historical Society*

local heroes. According to a newspaper account, Green wrote letters regularly to some 80 servicemen and gave a party for each Natick boy before he shipped out.

Thanks to the 1945 army-camp tours, as well as increased publicity in national magazines, a number of players in the women's league developed followings among servicemen in the United States and abroad. After she was pictured in the June 4, 1945, issue of *Life* magazine, center fielder Faye Dancer received a small parcel from a GI stationed in Denver. "Just a little package of gum," he wrote, "to help you win a few more ball games." The players received a more curious tribute in the September 1944 issue of *Esquire* magazine. Each month *Esquire* artist Varga drew a different version of his Varga pinup girl, a sexy woman meant to inspire the men who were fighting overseas. The monthly Varga Girl was accompanied by a poem, written by *Esquire* poet Phil Stack.

In September 1944, *Esquire* readers were treated to the Varga Girl in a tight, short baseball outfit, skimpier by far than the one approved by Philip Wrigley. Stack's poem, titled "All-American Babe," joked about adding a woman to the ranks of teenage boys who suddenly found themselves playing in baseball's major leagues. But it also seemed to acknowledge the athletic yet "feminine" players of what Wrigley now called the All-American Girls Professional Ball League (AAGPBL):

> *"All-American Babe"*
> The war has made some changes
>   In our nation's fav'rite game.
> For 'teen age kids are making
>   A bid for baseball fame.
> And though these "All-American Boys"
>   Will star as sure as fate,
> We'll add an "All-American Babe"
>   And overflow the gate!

Whether or not Stack was aware of the AAGPBL, his assumption about the appeal of women ball players was accurate. The league's four teams attracted 176,612 fans in 1943, and when Wrigley added two more teams the following year, attendance rose accordingly. In 1945 a total of 450,313 people paid 74 cents each (25 cents for children) to watch the Daisies, Chicks, Peaches, Belles, Comets, and Blue Sox play ball. What's more, in at least one city, the women's game proved more popular than men's baseball. A 1945 study compared the paid attendance at the games of the Fort Wayne Daisies—a new women's club transplanted from Minneapolis—and a local men's semipro baseball team. While the Daisies attracted an average of 1,245 paying fans per night, attendance at the men's contests (at only 50 cents per ticket) never topped 800, and was hovering around 100 by the end of the season. The women's game might not "overflow the gate," but in the Daisies' first season, it clearly was the game of choice in Fort Wayne.

By 1945 the outlook for the All-American Girls league was positive enough to ensure that this wartime phenomenon would continue beyond the war. But it would have to do so without its founder. In the fall of 1944, when the Allies finally seemed to be winning in Europe and major league baseball seemed destined to regain its prewar popularity, Philip Wrigley sold the women's league to his advertising director, Arthur Meyerhoff. Meyerhoff went on to serve as AAGPBL commissioner from 1945 through 1950, directing the league's affairs during its most successful period.

With the immediate future of the league secure, the AAGPBL led the celebrations when World War II finally drew to a close. The end came when Japan formally surrendered on August 14, 1945. (The Germans had surrendered three months earlier, on May 7.) "We were playing in Kenosha," remembered Rockford Peaches outfielder Jo Lenard. "I think we played one inning or so, and then a big crowd came in. They brought a little cannon and they fired it off, and then all heck broke loose. We were going to play in Grand Rapids the next day, and every time I went through Chicago, I'd call my mom and dad. This time I didn't even remember to do that."

On August 15, 1945, reporter Jim O'Brien, who covered the AAGPBL for the *Racine Journal-Times*, reflected in print on the end of the world's most devastating war. "As this is written in the small hours of the morning, there is probably little interest in yesterday's baseball scores," O'Brien wrote. "The final score on a bigger game has just come in, and the hometown team won." O'Brien went on to chronicle some of the more bizarre developments that American sports fans had witnessed during the war, from "sixteen-year-old boys and 50-year-old granddads" playing major league baseball to "college football teams staffed with high school boys who wouldn't have carried the water bucket in peacetime." He added, "Here in Racine, we even saw girls step out on the baseball diamond and play a game that fell somewhere between baseball and softball, and pack 'em in as few sports activities have in this city."

O'Brien didn't speculate on the effects that peace might have on the All-American Girls league. He just reported that "the boys in the know" predicted the United States was about to experience a great sports boom. But anyone who followed the women's games could guess that the AAGPBL would be part of that boom. Philip Wrigley's league had liberated a small army of female athletes and given them the chance to shine. Now that the war was over, they weren't about to stop.

Play Ball!

Max Carey played in the major leagues for 20 years, but he claimed the greatest baseball game he ever saw took place in the AAGPBL. The date was Monday, September 16, 1946; the place, Horlick Athletic Field in Racine, Wisconsin. The Racine Belles and the Rockford Peaches were nearing the end of a closely fought best-of-seven series for the league championship. Rockford was behind in the series, three games to two. If the Peaches lost game six, the Belles would take the title. More than 5,600 fans came out to watch Racine's Joanne Winter take the mound against Rockford's Carolyn Morris.

Winter and Morris were two of the league's All-Star hurlers. The game promised to be a pitching duel. But Winter had pitched in 50 games since the season opened, and the strain was beginning to show. When she served up a clean single to Rockford's first batter, Dorothy Kamenshek, it was the start of a 13-hit barrage by the Peaches. "Joanne was not in trouble occasionally," reported the *Racine Journal-Times.* "She was in trouble all the time." Indeed, before the 14-inning contest was over, Rockford would load the bases three times and advance players to third base six times. But the Belles' clutch fielding kept the Peaches from scoring.

Racine's fans watched in frustration as the Belles saved run after run only to have their own bats silenced. Peaches pitcher Morris was throwing one of her best games ever. "Carolyn Morris missed immortality in the Girls League records for lack of a run," reported the *Journal-Times*. "Carolyn pitched a no-hit game for nine innings, but failed to get the support at the plate that would have written the league's most important no-hitter into the record books." The game went into extra innings with the score tied 0–0.

In the bottom of the tenth, the Belles finally tagged Morris for two singles, only to have the Rockford pitcher shut them down. In the eleventh, the Peaches nearly broke the deadlock. Rockford got its first three batters on base, but Winter got out of the inning, thanks to a pop up, a force-out at home, and a grounder to first. In the bottom of the twelfth, it was Racine's turn to threaten. Base-stealing champ Sophie Kurys led off with a single to center, then quickly stole both second and third. When Morris hit the next batter, Peaches skipper Bill Allington replaced her with hurler Mildred Deegan. Deegan walked catcher Pepper Paire intentionally and, as Racine fans looked on in agony, managed to mirror Winter's accomplishment by escaping from the inning without giving up a run. But Racine had come within one base of scoring. They were beginning to taste victory.

When Kurys returned to the plate in the fourteenth, she again singled, this time through the left side of the infield. Then shortstop Moe Trezza came up to bat. As soon as Deegan delivered her first pitch, Kurys broke for second, successfully capturing her fifth stolen base of the night. There was one out and the winning run was in scoring position. The Rockford infield moved in for an expected bunt, but Trezza fooled them and drove a sharp grounder into right field. Kurys was off with the crack of the bat. She raced around third and dove for home. "It was an awful slide," remembered Joanne Winter, but it did the trick. When the dust settled, the Belles had won the game 1–0 and with it the championship.

That 1946 play-off game delivered a resounding message to the sports world: These women were serious about baseball. Maybe the AAGPBL was started to satisfy baseball fans during World War II, but the war had ended more than a year before, and the league had taken on a life of its own. The ball

◆ Belles play-off heroes Betty "Moe" Trezza and Sophie Kurys (sliding) pose for a publicity photo. *From the Collection of the Northern Indiana Historical Society*

RACINE VS. ROCKFORD
PLAY-OFF GAME
SEPTEMBER 16, 1946

Racine Belles	At-Bats	Runs	Hits	RBIs
Sophie Kurys, 2b	5	1	2	0
Moe Trezza, ss	5	0	1	1
Pepper Paire, c	4	0	0	0
Edie Perlick, lf	5	0	0	0
Eleanor Dapkus, cf	5	0	1	0
Maddy English, 3b	5	0	1	0
Marnie Danhauser, 1b	5	0	0	0
Betty Emry, rf	5	0	0	0
Joanne Winter, p	5	0	0	0
Totals	**44**	**1**	**5**	**1**

Rockford Peaches	At-Bats	Runs	Hits	RBIs
Dorothy Kamenshek, 1b	7	0	4	0
Dottie Ferguson, 2b	5	0	2	0
Lee Surkowski, cf	7	0	1	0
Naomi Meier, lf	5	0	2	0
Dorothy Harrell, ss	5	0	1	0
Rose Gacioch, rf	6	0	1	0
Velma Abbott, 3b	7	0	1	0
Dorothy Green, c	5	0	1	0
Carolyn Morris, p	4	0	0	0
Mildred Deegan, p	1	0	0	0
Totals	**52**	**0**	**13**	**0**

Score by Innings:

		Runs	Hits	Errors
Rockford 000 000 000 000 00		0	13	1
Racine 000 000 000 000 01		1	5	2

Errors—Abbott, Dapkus, English. **Left on base**—Rockford, 19; Racine, 6. **Triple**—Gacioch. **Stolen bases**—Kamenshek, Meier, Ferguson, Surkowski, Kurys (5), Winter. **Hit batters**—By Winter, Morris; by Morris, Trezza. **Time**—2:40. **Attendance**—5,630.

Racine	Innings	Hits	Runs	Walks	Strikeouts
Winter, W	14	13	0	4	4

Rockford	Innings	Hits	Runs	Walks	Strikeouts
Morris	11	3	0	1	8
Deegan, L	3	2	1	1	3

players did not follow in the footsteps of the Rosie the Riveters who left their wartime factory jobs when American soldiers and sailors came home. Under the direction of Arthur Meyerhoff and Max Carey, the All-American Girls Professional Baseball League did its best to carve out a place in the postwar sports scene.

Games in the women's league offered all of the excitement of men's baseball, and then some. The 1946 play-off battle between the Belles and the Peaches was just one of many contests that kept fans on the edges of their seats. Since managers tended to pit their best pitchers against each other, extra-inning games were not uncommon. Muskegon Lassies pitcher Doris "Sammy" Sams remembered when her manager named her to start the short game of a doubleheader against Rockford's Lois Florreich. (In the AAGPBL, doubleheaders included one nine-inning game and one "short," or seven-inning, contest.) By drawing the seven-inning game, Sams thought she'd gotten off easy. Instead, she and Florreich battled to a tie through the seventh inning and kept up the contest until the twenty-second, when Sams finally won. Sams remembered, "After that, I told my manager, 'I don't want to pitch any more seven-inning games. They're too long!' "

While many games were memorable for their impressive pitching or hitting, some stood out for more unusual reasons. Racine first baseman June Peppas remembered one game that the Belles played against the Peoria Redwings. "We were down by two runs in the eighth inning," said Peppas, "but our pitcher and Sophie Kurys had gotten on base. I was up next, with runners on first and second, and I connected with a pitch that went into the center-field stands." Peppas's home run should have added three runs to the Belles' total, putting them ahead of the Redwings. But the Redwings' center fielder was Faye Dancer, a fast-talking, crowd-pleasing favorite. "Faye convinced the umpire that my ball had *bounced* into the stands," said Peppas, "and he gave me a ground-rule double." On a ground-rule double, all runners automatically advance only two bases. "We scored only one run and lost the game. Later that evening, we had dinner at the same restaurant Faye was in, and she came over and apologized for robbing me of a fine home run. It took me the rest of the summer to get over that one."

Not surprisingly, umpires in the league figured in their share of questionable calls. When the calls affected the outcome of a game, the carefully coached "feminine" ball players could prove themselves as explosive as any major league male. An account of a 1948 game between the Rockford Peaches and the South Bend Blue Sox reported that South Bend first baseman Betty Whiting "kicked dust on the umpire's blue suit" when she was called out on strikes. After the umpire threw Whiting out of the game, South Bend's Jean Faut "aimed a kick at [his back], but was far enough away not to connect." Unfortunately, the umpire turned and saw Faut's foot in the air and tossed her out of the game too. A 1952 article on a Grand Rapids Chicks game reported that "Inez Voyce, usually a very placid first baseman, went berserk during a rhubarb with Al Stover, the home umpire, and took a swing at him." Voyce was miffed because Stover said she'd missed home plate after she thought she'd scored the Chicks' winning run.

By 1952, Inez Voyce's competitive spirit wasn't the only thing about the AAGPBL that brought the major leagues to mind. The rules of the game had evolved to be much more like those of regulation baseball. The game that Wrigley introduced in 1943 was a slightly faster version of softball, with base stealing, underhand pitching, a 12-inch ball, 65-foot base paths, and a 40-foot distance from the pitcher's mound

◆ Merle "Pat" Keagle argues a call with umpire Gadget Ward as catcher
Dottie Naum stands by. *National Baseball Library, Cooperstown, N.Y.*

to home plate. But the big ball was difficult to hit far, giving
the pitcher the edge. To heighten fan interest, league officials
shrunk the circumference of the ball to 11 inches in 1946, 10
inches in 1949, and 9 inches—major league baseball size—in
1954. They also changed the style of delivery, allowing either
underhand or sidearm pitching in 1946, only sidearm pitching in 1947, and overhand or sidearm pitching from 1948 on.
Meanwhile, the league also lengthened the pitching distance
and the distance between bases.

These changes speeded up the action and gave batters a chance to shine. Before the league allowed overhand pitching, no more than two players had batting averages higher than .300 in a single season, and no one could beat the .332 mark set in 1943 by Rockford shortstop Gladys "Terrie" Davis. Once overhand pitching took hold, the league saw six to eight .300 hitters each year, with the leader usually hitting in the .340s. And in 1954, Fort Wayne Daisies right fielder Joanne Weaver hit an amazing .429. That is three points higher than the best season batting average of any major leaguer in the twentieth century.

Although the changes in the AAGPBL game helped batters excel, they short-circuited some pitchers' careers. Rather than adapting their delivery style, a few underhand pitchers left the AAGPBL to return to fast-pitch softball. Others, including Connie Wisniewski, the league's first Player of the Year, gave up pitching to play other positions. Those who did convert to overhand pitching found the process a challenge. "I worked out in a gym all winter," remembered Joanne Winter. "Leo Murphy, our manager, was good enough to watch me. Leo helped me with holding runners on base, perfecting the delivery." In 1948, Winter's hard work paid off. That year she led the league in games won, becoming the only woman to do so as both an underhand and an overhand pitcher. (She shared the all-time underhand record of 33 wins with Wisniewski and the all-time overhand record of 25 wins with Alice Haylett.)

As the AAGPBL's game evolved, the league found itself with a problem: It no longer had a reliable source of new players. In the early years, most of the women who became All-Americans were softball stars, but now the teams were playing a game that was more like baseball than softball. Since relatively few women in the United States or Canada

◆ Racine hurler Joanne Winter, before the league switched to overhand pitching. *From the Collection of the Northern Indiana Historical Society*

grew up playing baseball, AAGPBL officials had two choices. They could continue to hire softball players and give them a chance to adjust to the faster style of ball. Or they could develop their own sources of new baseball talent. Meyerhoff and Carey did both. From 1946 through 1948, they scheduled increasingly ambitious spring-training programs so the women could practice before the regular season began. In 1949 and 1950, they added two "rookie" teams, whose players spent the summer honing their skills as they held exhibition games throughout the eastern United States. And starting in 1947, they helped league towns set up "junior" baseball programs that taught girls 14 and older to play the AAGPBL game.

Spring training and the rookie touring teams had the added benefit of introducing the league to audiences outside the Midwest. The women trained in Pascagoula, Mississippi, in 1946; Havana, Cuba, in 1947; and Opalocka, Florida, in 1948. And the touring teams made a loop from Chicago to Oklahoma City, New Orleans, Atlanta, New York City, Pittsburgh, and Indianapolis, with lots of stops in between. Spurred by newspaper articles and ads, local fans came out in force to watch the women play. In Cuba the AAGPBL attracted more spectators than the Brooklyn Dodgers, who also held their 1947 spring training there. The All-Americans "became the rage of all baseball-mad Cuba," reported the official account of the league's 1947 season. "Hundreds turned out to see them practice. And no less than 55,000 wildly enthusiastic fans watched the round-robin tournament which concluded the training program."

League officials were on the lookout for new talent wherever they went. The rookie teams held tryouts for local women in most towns, adding promising players to the tour or sending them to the Midwest to join the regular teams. And

◆ Players practice bunting during spring training, late 1940s. *From the Collection of the Northern Indiana Historical Society*

when the women left Havana in 1947, they took one of Cuba's top female ball players with them. Eulalia Gonzales, nicknamed "Viyalla," or "the Smart One," was the first of several Cubans recruited by the All-Americans.

Although the league welcomed the Cubans, no African-American women ever played in the AAGPBL. Two African-Americans did work out with the South Bend Blue Sox in May 1951, and in November of that year the league's Board of Directors debated the issue of integration at length. According to the minutes of the meeting, "The consensus of the group seemed to be against the idea of colored players, unless they would show promise of exceptional ability." The directors added that if any teams did hire an African-American player, "none of the clubs would make her feel unwelcome." Had the AAGPBL scouted African-American women, they would have found an abundance of talented ball players, including second baseman Toni Stone. In 1953, Stone became the only woman ever to play in the top level of the segregated Negro leagues, batting .243 in about 50 games with the Indianapolis Clowns.

The directors' decision to shy away from integration reflected attitudes in men's sports at the time. Before Jackie Robinson joined the Brooklyn Dodgers in 1947, African-American men could play top-level baseball only in the Negro leagues. And no African-American played in the National Basketball Association until Charles Henry Cooper joined the Boston Celtics in 1950. But the directors had more to consider than the progress of integration in other professional leagues. The AAGPBL was already breaking one social barrier by trying to convince the public to accept *women* as baseball players. It is likely that the directors were worried about the economic effects of challenging another barrier at the same time. In the late 1940s and early '50s, more and more AAGPBL teams were running up against money problems. They couldn't take any risks that might result in lower game attendance or negative publicity for the league. Welcoming African-American women was one such risk.

Thanks to Arthur Meyerhoff, the women players were earning quite a bit of positive publicity, including praise from some major league admirers. When Philadelphia Athletics manager Connie Mack saw quick-handed shortstop Dottie Schroeder in action, he declared, "If that girl were a man, she'd be worth $50,000 to me." And former New York Yankees first baseman Wally Pipp called Dorothy Kamenshek "the fanciest-fielding first baseman I've ever seen, man or woman." Soon after Pipp made his comment, the Fort Lauderdale team of the men's Florida International Baseball League tried to buy Kamenshek's contract from the AAGPBL.

◆ Seven-time All-Star Dorothy Kamenshek. *National Baseball Library,*
Cooperstown, N.Y.

She wasn't interested. "I'd never play in a men's league," she said at the time. "A woman would be at a physical disadvantage competing with men standing over six feet tall and outweighing her by 60 or 70 pounds."

Kamenshek's sentiments echoed those of the league's founder and the officials who came after him. Wrigley's goal had been to convince the public of the unique appeal of the women's game, emphasizing the players' "femininity" as much as their athletic skill. Like women's tennis in later years, the AAGPBL sought to have fans evaluate its product on its own merits, not by comparing it with the game played by men. Fred Leo, president of the league after Max Carey, summarized this point of view in 1950. "This is a girls' game, and our girls are not imitating men," Leo said. "It would simply be carnival stuff if we played one of our teams against men. . . . We are not interested in a meaningless competition with men. We are interested in showing a million people a year—and I hope it will turn into two million—that young women can put on a fine ball game all by themselves."

Indeed, the AAGPBL did put on fine ball games, and some of the players were stars by any standard. Dorothy Kamenshek was a prime example. During her ten-year career, she was elected to the league's All-Star team a record seven times, led the league in fielding once and batting twice, and was thought by many to be the AAGPBL's finest all-around player. But she had company at the top. Sophie Kurys set league marks by stealing 1,114 bases in her 914-game career, and an incredible 201 out of 203 attempts in 1946 alone. Pitcher/outfielder Doris Sams hurled a perfect game in 1947, captured the league's home run mark in 1952, hit above .300 every season from 1950 through 1953, and was elected Player of the Year in both 1947 and 1949.

There were other power hitters. Outfielder Audrey Wagner

of the Kenosha Comets was one of the first. Only 15 years old when she joined the league in 1943, Wagner held records during the 1940s for most hits (130), most extra-base hits (41), and most doubles (25) in a season. When overhand pitching was introduced in 1948, Wagner responded by leading the league in hitting and taking Player of the Year honors. In the 1950s, sisters Betty Weaver Foss and Joanne Weaver tore up the AAGPBL with their hitting, monopolizing the batting titles and many other hitting marks from 1950 through 1954. "Betty Foss and Jo Weaver were so strong, they could bunt the ball for a home run," remembered Grand Rapids Chicks catcher Marilyn Jenkins. "I used to hate to pitch to Betty Foss," added Ruth Williams. "Sometimes she'd tear my head off."

South Bend pitcher Jean Faut was another standout. From 1946 through 1953, Faut notched two perfect games, won Player of the Year honors twice, and had an eight-season earned run average of 1.23. "What a pitcher she was," remembered her catcher, Shirley Stovroff. "She had such good control. It was like sitting in a rocking chair back there. Wherever I put the glove, the ball was there." Arguably the best overhand pitcher in the league, Faut also had the distinction of being the only player who was married to her manager. Faut's husband, Karl Winsch, was a pitcher whose major league career had been cut short when he injured his arm. He managed the Blue Sox from 1951 through 1953, leading them to two league championships.

Faut and Winsch had a son, Larry, who was born before the start of the 1948 season. As a wife and mother, Faut had to juggle family responsibilities and her baseball career. But even those players who didn't have husbands or children found that life between ball games could be pretty hectic. Teams played an average of 112 games each season, with hardly any days off for rest or travel. After ball games, practices, and all-night road trips, the women had little free time. Yet the all-consuming nature of the league seemed to strengthen the bonds between the players and increase their dedication to the game. It made life in the league intense, and tiring, and sometimes, a whole lot of fun.

AAGPBL DREAM TEAM LINEUP

(Based on individual records and selections
as All-Stars or Players of the Year)

Pitcher (Overhand)
JEAN FAUT
South Bend, 1946–1953
5'4", 137 lb.
Bats right, throws right
Born January 17, 1925
Red Hill, Pennsylvania
All-Star Teams: 4
Player of the Year: 1951, 1953
Lifetime E.R.A.: 1.23
140 Wins; 64 Losses
Highlights: Pitched two perfect games; often played third base or outfield when she wasn't pitching.

★ AAGBL ★

JEAN FAUT
Pitcher

**Pitcher (Underhand)/Outfield
CONNIE "Iron Woman"
WISNIEWSKI**
Milwaukee/Grand Rapids,
1944–1949; 1951–1952
5'10", 147 lb.
Bats left, throws right
Born February 18, 1922
Detroit, Michigan
All-Star Teams: 5
Player of the Year: 1945
Lifetime E.R.A.: 1.48
107 Wins; 48 Losses
Lifetime Batting Average: .275
Highlight: Shares the pitching
record for most wins (33) in
a season with Joanne Winter.

CONNIE WISNIEWSKI
Pitcher — Outfield

RUTH RICHARD
Catcher — Outfield

**Catcher
RUTH "Richie" RICHARD**
Grand Rapids, 1947
Rockford, 1948–1954
5'4", 130 lb.
Bats left, throws right
Born September 20, 1928
Argus, Pennsylvania
All-Star Teams: 6
Lifetime Batting Average: .241
Highlight: Caught back-to-back
no-hit, no-run play-off games.

**First Base
DOROTHY "Kammie"
KAMENSHEK**
Rockford, 1943–1951, 1953
5'6", 136 lb.
Bats left, throws left
Born December 21, 1925
Cincinnati, Ohio
All-Star Teams: 7
Lifetime Batting Average: .292
Highlights: Struck out only
81 times in 3,736 times at bat;
batted .345 in 1951.

DOROTHY KAMENSHEK
First Base

SOPHIE KURYS
Second Base

**Second Base
SOPHIE "Flint Flash" KURYS**
Racine, 1943–1950
Battle Creek, 1952
5'5", 120 lb.
Bats right, throws right
Born May 14, 1925
Flint, Michigan
All-Star Teams: 4
Player of the Year: 1946
Lifetime Batting Average: .260
Lifetime Stolen Bases: 1,114
Highlights: Stole 201 bases
in 203 attempts in 1946;
during her career, stole at least
one base 80 percent of the
time she got on base.

Shortstop
DOROTHY "Dottie" SCHROEDER
South Bend;
Kenosha; Fort Wayne;
Kalamazoo, 1943–1954
5'8", 145 lb.
Bats right, throws right
Born April 11, 1928
Sadorus, Illinois
All-Star Teams: 3
Lifetime Batting Average: .211
(Improved steadily from
.188 in 1943 to .304 in 1954)
Highlights: Hit 17 home runs
in 1954; played every year
the league existed, then joined
Allington's All-Stars.

DOROTHY SCHROEDER
Shortstop

AUDREY WAGNER
Outfield

Outfield
AUDREY WAGNER
Kenosha, 1943–1949
5'7", 147 lb.
Bats right, throws right
Born December 27, 1927
Bensenville, Illinois
All-Star Teams: 2
Player of the Year: 1948
Lifetime Batting Average: .254
Highlights: Known as a power
hitter; used the money she
earned playing ball to go
to medical school.

Outfield/Pitcher
DORIS "Sammy" SAMS
Muskegon/Kalamazoo,
1946–1953
5'9", 145 lb.
Bats right, throws right
Born February 2, 1927
Knoxville, Tennessee
All-Star Teams: 5
Player of the Year: 1947, 1949
Lifetime Batting Average: .290
Lifetime E.R.A.: 2.16
64 Wins, 47 Losses
Highlights: All-around All-Star;
pitched a perfect game
in 1947.

★ *AAGBL* ★

DORIS SAMS
Pitcher — Outfield

Outfield
JOANNE WEAVER
Fort Wayne, 1950–1954
6'0", 145 lb.
Bats right, throws right
Born 1936
Metropolis, Illinois
All-Star Teams: 1
Player of the Year: 1954
Lifetime Batting Average: .359
Highlight: Batted .429 in 1954,
higher than any major leaguer
in the twentieth century.

Third/First Base
BETTY "Metropolis Mauler"
WEAVER FOSS
Fort Wayne, 1950–1954
5'10", 162 lb.
Bats left, throws right
Born May 10, 1929
Metropolis, Illinois
All-Star Teams: 1
Player of the Year: 1952
Lifetime Batting
Average: .340*
(*1954 statistics not available)
Highlight: Touted by Fort
Wayne as "Girls Baseball's
answer to the ATOM BOMB"
because of her
"explosive power."

◆ *Baseball cards courtesy of AAGBL Cards*
Weaver and Weaver Foss photographs from the Collection
of the Northern Indiana Historical Society

Life in the League

In 1946 and '47, the most promising rookies on the Racine Belles quickly learned that baseball skill wasn't the only thing they needed to survive in the AAGPBL. They also had to pass a test devised by catcher Pepper Paire and her teammates. Just outside of Racine there was a cemetery that had a particularly spooky tombstone. "When your headlights shined on the tombstone at a certain angle," remembered Paire, "it looked like it was rising right up off the ground." The veteran Belles put this apparition to good use. "We'd get the rookies, go out, have dinner, and at about midnight take them for a ride on the outskirts of town," Paire said. "We'd tell them, 'You've got to see this.' Then we'd turn into the cemetery and say, 'You've got to get out of the car, right at this spot.' Well, when they got out, we'd take off. They would usually stand there for about two minutes, because they didn't think we'd really leave them. But then they'd hear us pick up speed going the other way, and man, they'd start running. We figured if they could catch the car, they were fast enough to make the team."

◆ Rookie welcoming committee. From left to right, veteran Racine Belles Maddy English, Pepper Paire, Sophie Kurys, Marnie Danhauser. *Collection of Sue Macy*

Pepper Paire's initiation rite was a memorable, and appropriate, introduction to the All-American Girls Professional Baseball League. It gave newcomers the message that the league was more than just a series of baseball games. Before they could gain the veterans' acceptance, rookies had to prove they had the stuff real ball players were made of, both on the field and off. Coming up against the "tombstone tryout" was also a peculiar kind of honor. "We only did it to the ones we liked," said Paire. "We wouldn't terrorize anybody else." It was the final hurdle for players bold enough to seek a place in the exclusive community of women baseball pros.

If the veteran players were careful about the newcomers they embraced, it was because their community was special to them. The league gave the players a rare chance to form bonds with other women as friends, teammates, advisors, and co-

conspirators. For four months every year the women worked together, traveled together, and lived together, in hotels when they were on the road and in private homes in their team cities. They grew to trust each other and depend on each other. Although similar institutions existed in the military— the Army Nurse Corps, for one—the AAGPBL was unique in civilian life. And the women knew it. While other women their age followed the prescribed route to marriage and motherhood, the All-Americans took a detour and got to know each other, and themselves. It's not surprising that decades after the league folded, when the players' fastballs had slowed and their home-run swings had faded, their friendships had grown stronger than ever.

The AAGPBL community was all the more important because many of the players were living away from home for the first time. More than two thirds of the women joined the league when they were 17 to 22 years old. The adjustment was harder for some than for others. Twenty-year-old Earlene "Beans" Risinger left Hess, Oklahoma, to try out for the league in 1947, but she was so homesick when she reached Chicago that she caught the first train back to Hess. "I had never been more than a hundred miles away from home," said Risinger, who conquered her fears in 1948 to begin a seven-year stint as an All-American. Delores "Dolly" Brumfield was only 14 when she joined the South Bend Blue Sox, but for her, playing ball was one big adventure. Since Brumfield was so young, the Blue Sox asked married outfielder Daisy Junor to look after her. "When we were flying back from spring training in Havana, the plane hit an air pocket and fell several hundred feet," remembered Brumfield. "And I said, 'Hey, that was fun. Let's do that again.' " She looked over to find Junor clutching the arm of her chair, ready to throw up.

In team cities, league officials arranged to have groups of players rent rooms from families whose houses were within walking distance of the ballpark. Living in people's homes helped to ease the way for the homesick players, and provided some degree of supervision for the younger ones. "A lot of those people practically adopted the girls," remembered pitcher Fran Janssen. "They'd treat you like a member of the family." Chaperones had to approve all host families, and players needed their chaperone's permission if they wanted to change homes. "The people were just so super to us," said South Bend's Elizabeth "Lib" Mahon. "I mean, this one person I lived with, if I'd leave a pair of dirty socks around, I'd have to hide them, 'cause she'd have them washed before I got back to them. That's how good they were to us."

The warmth and generosity of the host families helped the players cope with their grueling schedule of daily ball games and frequent road trips. Each team averaged 25 to 35 trips per season between league cities, not including spring training and the championship play-offs. Since the league didn't schedule days off for travel, teams usually finished up their games in one town and immediately boarded trains or buses for the next. Although all of the AAGPBL's teams were located in the Midwest, the trips between some of the cities could be brutal. The Peoria (Illinois) Redwings had to drive almost 350 miles to Muskegon and Grand Rapids, Michigan, and about 325 miles to Fort Wayne, Indiana. In 1949, the Redwings traveled just under 7,000 miles in 34 trips during their 107-day season. On the average, they drove 206 miles every three days.

Players traveled by train during World War II, but once the war was over and the government stopped rationing gasoline, each team chartered its own bus. The buses gave the women privacy and a certain degree of comfort, but even the most luxurious coach couldn't eliminate the grind of constantly

◆ The 1949 rookie tour, with the bus the players rode during their 10,000-mile odyssey across the South, East, and Midwest. *Courtesy of Fran Janssen*

being on the road. "Many times we'd travel all night and get in about seven or eight o'clock in the morning," explained Dorothy Kamenshek. "We usually couldn't get our hotel rooms until noon, because they were occupied or they hadn't been cleaned yet, so we'd have breakfast and lounge around or go shopping. When we finally got into the rooms, we would sleep. But then we had to get up and go to the ballpark at about five P.M. to get ready for that night's game." In a 1982 survey, 99 former players were asked what they liked least about life in the AAGPBL. Thirty-nine percent agreed on travel. "I didn't dislike the travel," wrote Rockford shortstop Dorothy "Snookie" Harrell Doyle. "I hated it!"

While most players saw long bus rides as a necessary evil, they were less tolerant of their chaperones' insistence that they always dress in "feminine attire" when leaving the bus. "You couldn't get off the bus unless you put on a skirt," remembered infielder Joan Kaufman. "You'd travel all night long, and you'd be dead tired and have to go to the bathroom. They'd stop at a service station and nobody would be around, but you'd have to put a skirt on to get off the bus." Not surprisingly, some veterans found ways to beat the system. "I used to wear my raincoat," Jo Lenard admitted. "I'd have slacks on, but I'd roll them up to my knees and put the raincoat on top to go into the hotel."

Bus trips were least painful when players slept through them, but not many perfected that skill. Instead, they talked, did crossword puzzles, sang songs, or played charades or other games. "We played poker all the time," said pitcher Ruth Williams. "At South Bend, our bus driver built a poker table right into the bus. About six or seven people could fit around the table without any trouble. Once we were going from Grand Rapids to Peoria, and we just played poker the whole time. When we got off the bus and went into the hotel, we found out the rooms weren't ready. They let us go to the corner of a ballroom in the hotel, and we started playing again."

Poker playing probably wasn't one of the "feminine" pastimes Philip Wrigley had in mind when he developed the standards of behavior for his All-American Girls. But many of the league's chaperones were willing to look the other way. "I figured it was good and innocent and clean fun," said Helen Hannah, chaperone of the Muskegon and the Kalamazoo Lassies from 1947 through 1951. "If my kids were in their rooms playing cards, I knew damn well they weren't outside running around someplace, getting into

◆ Annabelle Lee and Tex Lessing check the sports page at the news-
stand in the Rockford Hotel, 1944. *From the Collection of the Northern
Indiana Historical Society*

some other kind of trouble." Still, Hannah took measures to
make sure her Lassies didn't gamble away too much cash.
Instead of giving them all of their meal money at the start
of a road trip, she doled it out during the trip, one day at
a time.

While most of the women spent their free time engaged in
"innocent and clean fun," a few made a practice of stretching
the rules to the breaking point. Faye Dancer, the center fielder
who robbed June Peppas of her game-winning home run,

could have written an encyclopedia of mischief. Dancer used to pry glass eyes out of horses on merry-go-rounds and give them to fans to rub for good luck. She regularly spent hours piecing together private letters that her teammates had ripped up and thrown away. Despite being an Episcopalian, she devotedly followed her Catholic friends into church so she could splash on some holy water, which she felt made her a better hitter. Dancer also remembered with pride the time she asked two players to wait in what she said was a teammate's car while she did an errand. They waited patiently, until a man came and asked what they were doing in *his* car. "People said to me, 'You must lie awake nights thinking these things up,' " Dancer said. "But I didn't. They just came naturally."

If her teammates had a hard time keeping up with Dancer, they weren't alone. Her antics bamboozled chaperones, managers, and even the league presidents. Dancer's most creative caper took place during spring training in 1944, her first year as a pro. She and Ann "Tootie" Harnett had gone to a bar for a few drinks and had stayed out past curfew, breaking two of the league's conduct rules. "Ken Sells, who was the president of the league before Max Carey, was in the hotel lobby with three chaperones," Dancer remembered. "We had to find a way to get up to the second floor without them seeing us." Dancer and Harnett headed to the back of the hotel, where they found some wooden beer kegs and a huge pile of coal. "We stacked two kegs on top of the coal," Dancer continued, "and I crawled up to the top of the kegs. Then I pulled myself up to the fire escape, and I helped Tootie up. The window near the fire escape was open, but it had a screen. While we were ripping the screen with a fingernail file, the elevator doors opened, and there were the president and the chaperones. We waited until they went into their rooms, and then we climbed in. They never caught us."

Behavior like Faye Dancer's was extreme, but it also re-flected the spirit and energy of the women in the league. "We needed some way to get the day's tensions and frustrations out," said Pepper Paire, who grew up with Dancer in Califor-nia and came east with her in 1944. For Paire and Dancer and many of the other players, unwinding after a tough game or a grueling road trip sometimes meant having a few drinks. "We couldn't drink in public places," Dancer remembered, "so in Fort Wayne we'd go out to the graveyard and drink beer and talk late into the night." In 1947 the league eased its rule on drinking, perhaps as an attempt to control the practice. Now the league would allow players to have "limited portions" of beer or wine, but "with after-game meals only."

Despite this change in the drinking rule, some players con-tinued to visit off-limits bars or drink with friends in private. Most of these women drank moderately. But those who went overboard could face serious consequences. In the 1940s and '50s, sports teams didn't provide counseling for players with alcohol problems. Instead, they tolerated—or ignored—the problem until it interfered with the player's ability to per-form. This was as true in major league baseball as it was in the AAGPBL. Excessive drinkers in the women's league could find themselves traded to other teams, or worse. One player later admitted that she was released from the league because of her drinking, and others may have suffered similar conse-quences.

For the most part, however, players made sure that their activities off the field didn't jeopardize their baseball careers. "The thing was that they were so involved in baseball," said chaperone Helen Hannah. "It didn't enter most of their minds to be rambunctious or boisterous or out of line." The punish-ing schedule of daily ball games made most players look forward to rest rather than excitement. A month or so into the

◆ Life on the road, 1947. Left to right: Mae Stark, Jenny Romatowski, Larraine Fisher, Marie "Blackie" Wegman. *Courtesy of Marie Wegman*

season, even the most dedicated athletes started to pray for rain-outs. When it was cloudy, All-Star Doris Sams was known to break out her fiddle and try to coax forth a rainstorm. And South Bend's Lib Mahon had her own favorite chant: "The farmers need the rain and the Blue Sox need the rest."

How did the women spend their time when it finally did rain? "Well, one thing we did was laundry," said Fran Janssen. Although the teams cleaned their players' uniforms, the women had to take care of their own shoes, gloves, and personal clothes. And unlike Lib Mahon's South Bend landlady, most host families stopped short of doing their boarders' wash. Besides heading for the washer and dryer, the women also used their free time to go shopping or go to the movies. And some of them went out on dates. "Any of us who wanted male companionship had no trouble finding it," remembered Pepper Paire. "The only thing was, we had a problem settling down. *I* didn't want to settle down. We were like sailors. We had different boyfriends in every town. I met a lot of wonderful guys. A lot of rich guys. But that was secondary. Baseball always came first."

In their team towns, the All-American Girls were celebrities. Men wined them and dined them. Business leaders sought their endorsements for their stores or products. Fans gave them gifts for hitting home runs or pitching shutouts. But if adults honored the women, children idolized them. When the Rockford Peaches started playing in 1943, Joan Kaufman was eight years old. "I used to live a couple of miles from the ballpark," Kaufman said, "and at night I could hear the announcer over the loudspeaker talking about the different players and what they were doing. I always wanted to be part of it." Like many girls in Rockford or South Bend or Fort Wayne, Kaufman was inspired by the women to play ball herself. In 1954, as the league began to fade into history, she finally joined the AAGPBL community, playing infield for the Peaches and winning recognition as Rookie of the Year.

CHAPTER 7

Hometown Heroes

Senaida "Shoo Shoo" Wirth was a scrappy South Bend shortstop who earned All-Star honors in 1946, her rookie year. The following spring *The A-A-G's Mail Bag* reprinted a letter to Wirth from the mother of a three-year-old Blue Sox fan. "We took Karen Ann to several of your games last summer," the mother wrote, "and of all the players on the field, you were the only one present as far as she was concerned. We have heard nothing but 'Shoo Shoo,' since she calls you on her play telephone and talks to you as if you were really there. You are included in everything she does. She sits you in a chair or on the davenport, and plays her piano for you, or sits and talks to you for hours. She throws the ball and says she's playing ball with Shoo Shoo. She'll say, 'Shoo Shoo, hit that ball!' You have really become my helper and nursemaid. If possible, I surely wish she could meet you as you are the only one in her world. If you care to come over to our home, you most surely are welcome as it seems you are already here."

It's not surprising that the *Mail Bag* chose to feature a letter celebrating Shoo Shoo Wirth's importance to a young fan. A good relationship between the players and their fans was crucial to the league's success. Without the fans' emotional— and financial—support, there could be no AAGPBL. In 1943, when Philip Wrigley spent $100,000 to start the league, business leaders in South Bend, Racine, Kenosha, and Rockford each added $22,500 of their own. But these investments would have gone to waste without backing from the general public. Fans had to come out and buy tickets to ball games. Local newspapers had to report on the women's games regularly and reliably. Like Karen Ann, people in league towns had to identify with their favorite players and the struggles of their teams.

Early on, league officials learned that teams had the best chance of developing strong followings if they were located in medium-sized cities, with populations of 50,000 to 175,000. Attempts in 1944 to start teams in Minneapolis, Minnesota (population 490,000 in 1940), and Milwaukee, Wisconsin (population 590,000 in 1940), failed. So did the addition in 1948 of a team in Chicago, Illinois (population 3,400,000 in 1940). Large cities offered too many choices for entertainment; the women's games couldn't catch on. Also, local newspapers, with lots of men's professional sports and other urban matters to cover, tended to be less interested in reporting on the AAGPBL.

In smaller cities like Racine (population 67,000 in 1940) and Rockford (population 85,000 in 1940), fans could get to know their players. Local papers ran articles on every game, usually with box scores and sometimes with photographs. Radio stations in South Bend, Fort Wayne, and some other cities featured play-by-play broadcasts of home games, and in 1950 a Rockford station also broadcast all of the Peaches' away games. Cities adopted the women's teams as their own, and local industries pointed to them with pride. "Hats off to

◆ Three team yearbooks, 1940s. Yearbooks tended to be about 60 pages long, and contained player photos and biographies, league statistics, summaries of the previous season, and ads. *From the Collection of the Northern Indiana Historical Society (South Bend and Muskegon); Collection of Sue Macy (Peoria)*

the Redwings," declared an ad for Caterpillar Inc. in the 1949 Peoria yearbook. "Win or lose—all Peoria is loyal to our Redwings. We like their spirit. We cheer their sparkling plays. Their will to win deserves our admiration. For they bring to our community a spirit of teamwork. And that's good for Peoria—good for all of America, too!"

Since the All-Americans lived with families in town, the athletes didn't seem as untouchable as the sports heroes in larger cities. Fans came to think of them as their neighbors or friends, even if they had never met. They celebrated the players' good fortune and helped out if things went bad.

◆ Muskegon Lassies (left to right) Doris Sams, Alva Jo Fisher, and Jo Lenard during a radio broadcast. *From the Collection of the Northern Indiana Historical Society*

When Rockford Peaches catcher Ruth Richard broke her ankle one season, fans surprised her with $600 that they had collected to pay for her medical expenses. But being a familiar part of strangers' lives made some players uncomfortable. "Being recognized frightened me," remembered slugger Dorothy Kamenshek. "At the beginning, a lot of the fans thought I was conceited or uppity because I'd never answer them when they spoke to me. But I was so shy, I didn't know what to say."

Although it came too late to help Kamenshek adjust to her fame, the league did make an effort to prepare players to deal with the public. In 1950 it issued *A Guide for All-American Girls*, an 11-page pamphlet full of tips on health, beauty care, and personal behavior. "Because you are a ball player and a member of the team in your home town city, it is taken for granted that you will be popular and well known by sight," the pamphlet said. "Both younger and older people will be interested in you and you will soon get over being surprised when strangers approach you and call you by your name. . . . Be as friendly and as gracious as you possibly can on these occasions. Your own personality represents your team and all of the girls in the All-American League. Don't be abrupt or rude to fans if you can possibly avoid it. Letting them feel that they know you, giving them a good impression through your speech and mannerisms, will help to make them regular and steady fans and will develop more 'customers' for the league and greater success for you personally."

For the most part, players followed this advice, gracefully accepting compliments and tactfully ignoring criticism from fans of opposing teams. Sometimes, ignoring critical fans took more than a little self-control. South Bend's Jean Faut remembered an incident in Fort Wayne when the home-plate umpire threw her out of the game after she made a heated

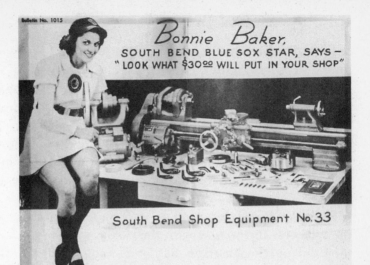

Bulletin No. 1015

Bonnie Baker,
SOUTH BEND BLUE SOX STAR, SAYS —
"LOOK WHAT $30.00 WILL PUT IN YOUR SHOP"

South Bend Shop Equipment No. 33

A LASSIE SPECIAL
A Real Saving
BEET SUGAR 10 lb. bag **99¢**

A LASSIE SPECIAL
Van Camp
GRATED TUNA 2 for **43¢**
Save 10%

A LASSIE SPECIAL
PILLSBURY—White, Yellow, Chocolate
CAKE MIX Your Choice. Box **33¢**
You save 5c per box

A LASSIE SPECIAL
WHITE HOUSE
COFFEE lb. **77¢**
You save 4c a pound

◆ Catcher Bonnie Baker appears in ads for South Bend Shop Equipment and a Kalamazoo, Michigan, grocery store. Baker is second from the top in the grocery store ad. Above her is pitcher Ruth Williams. *Courtesy of Ruth Williams Heverly*

remark. Faut left the field, walking through the box seats and up the steps that led out of the stadium to her team bus. "As I walked up the steps," she said, "one of the Fort Wayne fans, bless them, poured a pitcher of cold water over my head. I never turned around and just kept right on walking." Not everyone had Faut's discipline. Pepper Paire barely skipped a beat after a fan yelled, "I see you haven't gotten any smaller since last year" at her opening game one season. Paire yelled back, "I notice your mouth hasn't lost weight, either!"

Since the league depended on local support for its success, the women's interaction with the public went beyond what they did on the baseball diamond. Fans regularly invited players to picnics or barbecues. Local branches of the Lions, Kiwanis, and Rotary clubs held luncheons where the women were expected to mingle with club members. The league encouraged the women to attend these events. "Accept invitations or decline them with graciousness," said *A Guide for All-American Girls*. "You may have opportunities to attend local functions and whenever it is in the best interests of the team and league, make every attempt to cooperate." In the same spirit, players were encouraged to help out local businesses by endorsing their products free of charge. Catcher Bonnie Baker appeared in ads for a local supermarket and for South Bend Shop Equipment, posing enthusiastically with a vise and a lathe.

Although players weren't paid for their endorsements, merchants contributed to the league in other ways. In 1950, three businesses in Rockford, Illinois, promised cash prizes to Peaches who distinguished themselves during games. Hoffman & Son Jewelers and Optometrists awarded $2.00 to women who hit doubles; Mandt Brake Service gave $3.00 to those who hit triples; and Johnson & Burke Jewelers awarded $3.00 to pitchers who pitched shutouts and catchers who

◆ Matchbooks issued by two teams in the early 1950s. Team schedules were printed inside the covers. *Courtesy of Ruth Williams Heverly*

◆ Fan club membership card, 1953. *Courtesy of Carol Owens*

caught them, as well as $5.00 to players who hit home runs. Outstanding players also received money and gifts on their own special nights. On August 31, 1950, Alma "Gabby" Ziegler, pitcher, infielder, and captain of the Grand Rapids

Chicks, received "probably the most enthusiastic tribute paid to any athlete wearing Grand Rapids colors in modern sports history," according to the *Grand Rapids Press*. After the crowd of 2,251 spectators gave her a standing ovation, Ziegler was flooded with gifts. She received an electric roaster from the team's board of directors, a ten-dollar bill signed by the visiting Fort Wayne Daisies, and "pocketbooks and scores of cash gifts" from fans and merchants.

While league officials encouraged interaction between the players and their community, they cautioned the women about being too friendly or too trusting, especially with male fans. Goodwill was one thing; romantic or sexual involvement was quite another. The women were expected to stop just short of encouraging unwanted advances. "There is always a way in which a lady can politely avoid unwanted company or attention," said *A Guide for All-American Girls*. "If you conduct yourself as a lady at all times you will retain your own self respect and that of others." But determined fans could put players in some awkward situations. "One of the men on the board of directors of the Fort Wayne team asked me to be his live-in," remembered Tiby Eisen. "His wife had died, and he was all for buying me a Cadillac and setting me up. But I was in my early twenties then. I wasn't interested in any 65-year-old man."

Faye Dancer's splashy playing style inspired devotion from a wide variety of fans, among them the members of the local organized-crime mob in Peoria, Illinois. "They'd come to see us play in Kenosha and Racine," Dancer remembered. "Here would come this old blue Packard with bulletproof glass. The kingpin liked me. He gave two dinners for my parents, and a brunch. He offered to buy my folks a new car. He offered me a golden palomino, and he said he'd put me up in the sporting-goods business if I stayed in Peoria. I said, 'Never.'

◆ Cartoon from the *Peoria Star*, as displayed in Faye Dancer's scrapbook. Dancer placed a reprint of the cartoon in the upper right, where her picture originally appeared. *Courtesy of Faye Dancer*

Once he even asked me if I wanted anyone killed. I told him maybe the umpire, but I made sure he knew I was kidding."

Performing for 1,000 to 3,000 fans each night brought the women all kinds of adulation, but even the most ardent fans backed off when their advances were rejected. Relationships with sportswriters, however, weren't always so respectful. "There was a reporter in Grand Rapids who was always trying to date the ball players," remembered Chicks pitcher Larraine Fisher. "If you didn't go along, sometimes he would write sarcastically about you. Once I had made an error, and he printed that the ball went through my skinny legs. I told him he might think my legs were skinny, but that was his opinion and shouldn't be printed. He referred to me as 'Chubby' after that to get my goat."

If the All-American Girls league needed fans to survive, it also needed sportswriters to keep those fans informed. A steady stream of colorful, lively articles on league games could go a long way toward filling up a stadium. But almost all of the sportswriters were men, and they were used to reporting on the achievements of male athletes. When faced with the prospect of writing about the AAGPBL, some balked, unable to fully accept women playing the national pastime. These writers hardly ever recounted a game's highlights without including their own observations on the players' femininity. They slipped references to players' hair styles, slim figures, and "well-proportioned legs" into their articles. Yet few went so far as to harass players or bribe them with favorable write-ups in exchange for dates.

Most sportswriters reflected their cities' loyalty to the women's teams, praising their victories and bemoaning their losses. Some even turned to poetry after their team played a noteworthy game. On July 7, 1945, Annabelle "Lefty" Lee of the Fort Wayne Daisies pitched nine innings of no-hit, no-run ball against the Grand Rapids Chicks. Three days later, Grand Rapids reporter K. C. Clapp responded with the following update of Edgar Allan Poe's poem "Annabel Lee":

It wasn't so many hours ago
    July 7, specifically,
That a maiden there pitched whom you may know
    By the name of Annabelle Lee,
And she hurled so well that not a Chick hit,
    Going down to her, one, two, three.

She was not wild, this talented child,
    Who twirled so effectively.
And no free passes were handed out
    By this stingy Annabelle Lee
But the base hits rang for the Fort Wayne gang
    For a 6–0 victory.

And this is the reason as 3,000 know
    Who witnessed her wizardry
That not a Chick could hit a lick
    Off the slants of Annabelle Lee,
So they sharply dropped from second spot
    To a humble berth in 3.
But Fort Wayne cheers its peach-clad dears
    Because of Annabelle Lee.

The moon never beams without bringing me dreams
    Of the curves of Annabelle Lee.
And the South Field lights will gleam many nights
    Before such a sight I may see—
No hits by Ziegler or Tetzlaff or Eisen,
    No hits by the bustling "B."
No hits by Maguire or Petras or "Twi,"
    Why? Because of Annabelle Lee.

◆ Poet's muse Annabelle "Lefty" Lee. *From the Collection of the Northern Indiana Historical Society*

Inspired by this and other spirited tributes, fans came to the ballpark in force, encouraging officials to expand the league. The AAGPBL fielded six teams in 1944, eight teams in 1946, and 10 teams in 1948. During this time, the league's total paid attendance also grew, reaching an all-time high of 910,747 in 1948. What's more, from 1946 through 1949, at least four of the All-American Girls teams regularly drew more fans than the total populations of their cities—a sign of economic well-being in baseball circles.

Yet as the 1950s approached, there were hints that interest in the women's games had peaked. The Springfield (Illinois) Sallies, one of the two teams added in 1948, folded in the middle of the year. The other new team, the Chicago Colleens, closed down at the end of the season. League officials kept the clubs' names and their uniforms, creating the two rookie touring teams that operated in 1949 and 1950. But the

◆ Newspaper ad for a rookie touring team game, 1949. *Courtesy of Fran Janssen*

CALL UP YOUR FRIENDS
GET UP A PARTY —
COME TO THE BALL GAME —
HAVE A GOOD TIME

Admission
Adults $1.00
Children 50c

addition of these "farm teams" couldn't mask the fact that in 1949, for the first time ever, the AAGPBL fielded fewer teams than it had the year before.

During the league's lifetime, a total of ten teams either folded or moved to new towns because of financial problems. But fans didn't let their teams go without a fight. When the Grand Rapids Chicks faced hard times in 1950, a public fund drive raised $4,000—enough to convince team owners to keep the Chicks in business. That same year, Peoria fans responded to the Redwings' financial difficulties by donating more than $8,000, starting a fan club, and writing passionate letters urging community support. "I think it is a shame if Peoria doesn't have enough civic pride to keep the Redwings here," one fan wrote to the *Peoria Star* in July 1950. "There should be enough people in Peoria interested to help the cause for the sake of the town kids." The fans' letters and donations encouraged Peoria officials to stick with the Redwings through the 1951 season. Grand Rapids, together with Fort Wayne, South Bend, Rockford, and Kalamazoo, continued to play until the league folded after the summer of 1954.

CHAPTER

Going...Going...Gone

On April 5, 1955, Bill Kerr, secretary of the Fort Wayne Girls Ball Club, Inc., wrote a letter to club president Robert O'Brien. The letter did not include plans for spring training or news about the Daisies' rookie prospects. Instead, Kerr asked O'Brien to close out the bank account that the Daisies used to pay their players. Then he took inventory of what remained of the Daisies' dream. "We cleaned out the clubhouse last Saturday," wrote Kerr, "and all that is left of any value is: the P.A. system with a lot of records; the intercom system, which is in good shape and which we paid about $100 for; 133 folding seats, which cost us originally between $1,500 and $2,000; quite a number of pieces of worn-out canvas, with not too much value; the old home run fence, which I don't imagine anyone would pay us for; and miscellaneous odds and ends too numerous to mention—value about two broken bats." Once these items were sold or given away, Kerr would close the books on the Fort Wayne Daisies. At the same time, officials in Kalamazoo, South Bend, Rockford, and Grand Rapids were dismantling their own teams.

What happened to reduce the All-American Girls Professional Baseball League to a collection of public address systems, folding chairs, and closed bank accounts? Just as the developments of the early 1940s led to the beginning of the league, the events and trends of the early 1950s led to its end. In 1943 teams had a captive audience. People were stuck in their hometowns because of gas rationing, and they welcomed the women's games as patriotic, uplifting entertainment that took their minds off wartime fears. By the late 1940s the nation had readjusted to peacetime, and an extraordinary era of economic growth had begun. Americans suddenly had countless ways to spend their free time. They could take a drive in one of the 21 million new cars sold from 1946 through 1950. They could try their skill at one of the 52,500 bowling lanes built by 1950, or take in a movie at one of the 2,000 drive-in theaters that opened between 1947 and 1950.

Many of the Americans who did stay close to home in the years following the war spent time with a new diversion, television. Although TV was introduced to the public in the late 1930s, World War II slowed its development. In 1945 there were only nine television stations and fewer than 7,000 TV sets in the whole country. But that was about to change. In 1946, the National Broadcasting Company created the first TV network when it began televising regular series from New York City to Philadelphia and Schenectady, New York. In 1948 America fell in love with its first TV star, comedian Milton Berle. By 1949 there were a million television sets in the United States. Two years later, the total had shot up to 10 million.

Early TV shows were broadcast live, and that made sports a prime candidate for the tube. The unscripted excitement of a double play or a ninth-inning home run kept baseball fans glued to their sets. It was hard for primitive TV technology to capture the action of a baseball game—cameras either were

◆ Three viewers in Philadelphia watch the first coast-to-coast TV broadcast as President Harry S Truman addresses the United Nations in San Francisco, October 25, 1946. *Acme*

too close to show the entire field or too far away to show the details. But fans still welcomed the chance to watch ball games in the comfort of their own homes. In 1947 viewers on the East Coast could see the first televised World Series, between the New York Yankees and the Brooklyn Dodgers. By the early 1950s stations in many major league cities were broadcasting their teams' games on a regular basis.

Attendance at minor league baseball games suffered because of television. So did attendance at the women's games. "People would rather sit home and watch TV than make the effort to go out and watch a ball game," said Lib Mahon, who left the league after the 1952 season. "In 1953 I took my mother out to Playland Park in South Bend, and there were about seventy-five people in the stands. The business manager told me that they had to have fifteen hundred people at each home game to even pay the salaries of the players. Attendance really fell off." But television and other new leisure-time activities weren't the only factors that led to the end of the AAGPBL. Changing views about the role of women in society were responsible too.

During World War II, women had been called upon to serve their country by taking jobs that traditionally were held by men. They worked in factories making guns and ships. They flew newly built airplanes to army bases all over the United States. They worked as lumberjacks, barbers, butchers, and bus drivers. But as the war drew to a close, the government began a campaign to convince women to quit their jobs so returning war veterans could fill them. Suddenly national leaders charged that working mothers neglected their children and caused juvenile delinquency. The female dean of Barnard College claimed that women were not reliable employees because they had "less physical strength, a lower fatigue point, and a less stable nervous system" than men. Articles in women's magazines advised readers to let their husbands take over as heads of the household if they wanted their marriages to last.

Despite this campaign, one survey after another showed that the majority of women wanted to continue working. "War jobs have uncovered unsuspected abilities in American women," a female worker said in response to a 1946 survey. "Why lose all these abilities because of a belief that 'a woman's place is in the home'? For some it is, for others not." Yet women found their job opportunities shrinking fast. By the end of 1946, more than two million women had been fired from jobs in automobile plants, airplane factories, and other "heavy" industries. IBM and other companies brought back their prewar policies of not hiring married women at all.

Those women who did work had to settle for lower pay, and their choices often were limited to traditionally "female" fields such as teaching and secretarial work. As their options narrowed, women's attitudes toward employment began to change. Many came to believe they could contribute more as wives and mothers than as employees in the jobs that were still open to them. A family-centered lifestyle, with the woman as homemaker and the man as provider, became the postwar American ideal.

This focus on home and family also was a reaction to the growing sense of insecurity many people felt after the war. In 1945 the United States had unleashed the power of a new— and frightening—weapon when planes dropped atomic bombs over the Japanese cities of Hiroshima and Nagasaki. After the war Americans watched as Communism spread throughout Eastern Europe and Asia. They worried that the Communists, too, would develop "the bomb." The 1950 invasion of South Korea by forces from Communist North Korea seemed to confirm people's fears that world events were out of control. Many Americans reacted by focusing on the one thing they *could* control. They got married, bought houses, had children, and created their own safe, protective units, their families.

As Americans started to focus inward, the AAGPBL was increasingly out of step with the times. The league was still celebrating the athletic abilities of strong, independent women, but the country was more interested in women's roles within the family. "The league stopped basically because the members were so outside the so-called 'norm' for women in the fifties," said Carol Owens, a player on the Fort Wayne Junior Daisies who lost her chance to make the pros when the league folded. In the 1940s the ball players had symbolized the America that the boys overseas were fighting to protect. In

◆ With the slogan "Don't let Pearl Harbor happen to you," this 1951 Los Angeles "Bomb Shelter Mart" offers two different bomb shelter models for $795 each. *AP/Wide World Photo*

the 1950s the same women found themselves in what was now male territory.

League officials tried to reassure the public that its players were no threat to traditional values. Whenever possible, they shined the spotlight on stars who were also wives and mothers. Sometimes the press helped. A 1950 article on the AAGPBL in *McCall's* magazine was titled "Hey Ma, You're Out!" and featured a full-page photo of Jean Faut with her husband and son. A 1952 article in *Holiday* magazine included the story of Canadian pitcher Audrey Haine Daniels, whose husband had to miss one of her games because "he was busy trying to get 22-month-old daughter Marilyn to sleep in the back of the car." But occasional articles weren't enough to sell the All-American Girls to their newly conservative audience. Officials needed a publicity campaign on the same scale as the one that had successfully introduced women's baseball to the public in 1943.

By the 1950s, however, the AAGPBL no longer had the money or the leadership to mount an expensive publicity campaign. In 1951 team owners had voted to do away with the league's management organization, headed by Arthur Meyerhoff. This group had run spring training, the rookie tours, the scouting program, and special promotion and publicity events. By disbanding Meyerhoff's group, each team saved as much as $7,000 per year in membership fees—a lot of money for clubs that were strapped for cash. But now each team had to take care of its own scouting and publicity. Besides making it impossible to launch a full-scale publicity campaign, this decision had other consequences. Without Meyerhoff's group, the AAGPBL no longer had an efficient way to find new players or to train the rookies they chose. The softball players recruited by the league needed time and practice to adapt to the league's baseball rules. Instead of enjoying a long spring training or playing on a rookie tour, they had to crowd all of their practice into the two weeks before opening day.

Taken together, this change in the league's structure and the social and political developments after World War II spelled doom for the All-American Girls Professional Baseball League. "Financially, they really were having problems," remembered Joan Kaufman of the Rockford Peaches. "We never did get our last paychecks." The once powerful Peaches finished in the cellar in 1954, the only one of the five remaining AAGPBL teams not to make the play-offs. "After the last game of the season, a couple of players kept their uniforms,"

◆ Fort Wayne Daisies celebrate a victory, 1950s. *From the Collection of the Northern Indiana Historical Society*

said Kaufman. "They wouldn't turn them in until they got paid. I wish I had kept mine, because it would have been a nice memento. I think the cleaning company wound up with the uniforms."

For the record, the Fort Wayne Daisies finished at the top of the standings that last season, but the Kalamazoo Lassies beat them in the play-offs. Kalamazoo's win was even more impressive because Fort Wayne's manager was Bill Allington, skipper of the Rockford Peaches during their dynasty years.

Allington wasn't one to end his managing career with a loss. Although the AAGPBL folded, he was determined to keep women's baseball alive. He convinced some of the league's rising stars to join him on the All-American Girls Baseball Team, a barnstorming group that played exhibition games throughout the United States and Canada. "There were twelve of us altogether, counting Bill," remembered infielder Joan Berger. "We had two cars, Bill's station wagon and my two-door Ford. Each person took one suitcase. And we'd travel. Sometimes we had to drive three hundred miles, sometimes five hundred miles. We'd play from Memorial Day to Labor Day, the same as the league. It was a rough life."

Although the All-American Girls team borrowed its name from the AAGPBL, it didn't borrow its rules. The women's team usually played against men's teams in the towns they visited, something that the women's league strictly forbade. The barnstorming team also made the most of people's curiosity about women ball players. "Bill always told us you had to have a gimmick to draw people," Berger said. "We used to put on a little exhibition before the game, like infield practice. Or we did contests. We had one girl racing against a

◆ Bill Allington with the members of his All-American Girls Baseball Team, 1955. *From the Collection of the Northern Indiana Historical Society*

horse—Jo Weaver, she could run. And then we had [Dolores] 'Pickles' Lee pitching two balls at the same time with the same hand."

Allington and his team entertained baseball fans through the summer of 1958, playing in as many as 150 cities per season. But these talented All-Americans now had to rely on carnival tactics to get people out to the ball park. When the league folded, women baseball players once again became oddities. Women *softball* players were making great strides, but *baseball* was seen as a man's game, and only male players were taken seriously. By the late 1950s, female baseball players were as rare as riveters named Rosie. These sports pioneers had no choice but to find other outlets for their athletic abilities and competitive spirits.

Indeed, the women of the AAGPBL were so successful at getting on with their lives that their experiences as baseball pros were almost lost to history. For close to 30 years, many of the women kept quiet about the league, preferring obscurity to the insulting comments ("You played *base*ball? How cute!") and the curious stares. "I never told many people about it because in some ways I was ashamed," said catcher Shirley Stovroff. "We were going against society, with its rules and regulations telling us that this is the way we should grow up and this is what we should do. And therefore we did take a beating." But even as the players retreated to other lives, the memories remained. And finally, the world was ready to share them. "Now I realize I did something that a lot of women would give their eyeteeth to have done," said Shirley Stovroff. "I'm very proud of that moment in the sun, or whatever you want to call it. It was great for me. I'll never deny it or be ashamed of it again."

CHAPTER
9

Reclaiming the Past

Women and baseball," said Julie Croteau. "These are two perfectly nice words, that when put together sometimes really freak people out." Croteau knew what she was talking about. At age 20 she had spent most of her life fighting for the right to play baseball. In high school she sued her coach after he cut her from the boys' junior varsity team. In college she withstood three years of jeers and cruel jokes as the first woman to play baseball for a National Collegiate Athletic Association (NCAA) school. Now, on October 26, 1991, Croteau stood in front of some 160 former players of the All-American Girls Professional Baseball League, gathered for a reunion in Clearwater Beach, Florida. "Women and girls *can* play baseball, and they can play it well," Croteau said. "You are living proof of this. Your league was a phenomenal institution. You were not only ahead of your time, but apparently, you were ahead of ours."

Some 37 years after the league folded, it was clear that the women in Croteau's audience *were* ahead of their time, and not just on the baseball diamond. Their experiences in the league had helped them develop a spirit of independence that

carried over into their post-baseball lives. Now in their six-
ties, they were women who seemed comfortable with the
world and their place in it. They spoke with confidence. They
joked with each other easily. They carried themselves as if
they were used to having people treat them with respect. And
they were generous with their affection. When the women
applauded Croteau's words, they seemed more intent on encouraging her in her first public speech than on celebrating
their own accomplishments.

Playing in the league had given the women the chance to
test their physical and emotional limits, and in the process to
expand them. That set them apart from other women of their
day. The women of the AAGPBL were used to living their
lives on their own terms. Many of them resisted the suppor-
ting role of wife and helpmate. Those who married took a
more active part in providing for their families. Those who
didn't struck out on their own. "I think most of the women
who did play in the league are unusual women," said Tiby
Eisen, who became one of the first female equipment installers
with General Telephone in California. "Most of them were
very self-confident and knew what they could do, and they
were good and could produce. And I think they'd be the same
way on a job or any other thing."

Statistics help emphasize the degree to which the All-
American Girls forged their own paths. Overall, women who
grew to adulthood in the United States during and just after
World War II had the highest marriage rate of any generation
in the twentieth century. Just over 96 percent of those women
got married. Yet a 1982 survey of 103 AAGPBL players and
chaperones showed that only 47 percent of them married.
And even those players who did marry were not content to
stay home. Although 75 percent of the married players had
children, only 23 percent of that group listed their career as

◆ Former teammates Dottie Schroeder (left) and Tiby Eisen at the 1991 reunion in Clearwater Beach, Florida. *Photo by Sue Macy*

"homemaker." The others, like their unmarried colleagues, held jobs outside the home.

Many of the players channeled their energies into the "women's jobs" that were open to them—teaching, secretarial work, factory work, and the like. But the league also produced at least two medical doctors, three police officers, four military officers, five professional athletes in other sports, and one mechanical engineer. Slugger Audrey Wagner became a doctor. Faye Dancer and Pepper Paire went into electronics. Jean Faut became a professional bowler, and Joanne Winter a golf pro. Both Shirley Stovroff and June Peppas started their own printing businesses. Dorothy Ka-

◆ Faye Dancer, with her souvenirs of the AAGPBL, at the first national reunion in July 1982. *Photo by Sue Macy*

menshek became a physical therapist. "If you look at our history, you'll find that most of us were from either the rural or working class," said Dolly Brumfield, who earned a doctorate in physical education and became a professor at Henderson State University, in Arkansas. "We were not the elites of society. The league gave us a chance to get out of poverty and out of the working class."

The experience of being professional athletes gave many players the confidence to strive for better lives. "My mom was from Poland," said left fielder Jo Lenard. "She had no education. My dad only went to school through the fourth grade. After I was done playing ball, I had a few jobs. I worked in a sporting-goods store. Then I was able to get a playground job. When I was working at the playground, somebody talked me into going to college. Well, I'd been out of high school for twenty-five years, but I figured, everybody's talking about college. I'll go for six months, so I can say I went. I kept my full-time job—I worked from two thirty in the afternoon to nine thirty at night—and went to college in the mornings. It was tough, let me tell you." Despite her plan to spend only six months in school, Lenard stuck with it. After four and a half years, she graduated as a high school physical education and science teacher. She taught for 17 years before an injury forced her to retire.

The self-assurance that the women developed playing ball liberated them both socially and economically. It also liberated some of their fans. "The women were my heroes," said Fort Wayne junior player Carol Owens. "They were wonderful role models. I saw strong, risk-taking women as I grew up, and that helped me to know it was okay to be a strong, competitive, and risk-taking person myself." Owens, who joined the Navy and then went to college to become a teacher, was also encouraged because the players seemed to be accepted by their fans. "At a time when women were being pushed into stereotypical roles, these women were doing what they wanted," she said. "And their fans loved them. I don't ever remember anything but the women being treated with a great deal of respect and love."

Even though Carol Owens didn't play in the AAGPBL, the league had an impact on her life. But when it folded, the players' achievements faded from the public memory. Girls growing up after the 1950s no longer had the All-Americans

◆ Photo of Dottie Schroeder, framed by autographs of other players, in the scrapbook of junior player Carol Owens. *Courtesy of Carol Owens*

as role models. "When I first learned of your league, I was so impressed, and at the same time, really infuriated," Julie Croteau told the former players in 1991. "I'd been playing baseball for 13 years without a single mention of early women ball players, never mind professionals. I was mad because I had felt alone, which is okay when you are, but I wasn't. And I was mad for you ladies, because somewhere, somehow, you had been cheated out of your place in the history books and the baseball stories."

Croteau finally did learn about the AAGPBL because the players took steps to reclaim their past. The social climate in the United States had changed in the 1970s, as women increasingly sought more active roles in government, business, sports, and other areas. At the same time, writers and teachers began to celebrate women's contributions to history. By the early 1980s the All-Americans couldn't help but think of their own accomplishments. In 1980 a few former players decided to try and find out what had happened to their old teammates. Those inquiries led to a newsletter, a series of national reunions, and a plan for creating a permanent record of the league. The women started to put together a lifetime roster of players. They searched for a museum or library where they could deposit scrapbooks, letters, photographs, and other memorabilia. And they sought recognition in the National Baseball Hall of Fame, if not for individual players, at least for the league as a whole.

As a result of their efforts, the league started to attract national attention. In 1987 two documentaries made during a reunion were shown on public TV. In 1988 the Northern Indiana Historical Society, in South Bend, offered to house the AAGPBL's official archives. A few months later, the National Baseball Hall of Fame dedicated its permanent "Women in Baseball" exhibit. Among the spectators at the Cooperstown dedication was Penny Marshall, who had seen one of the documentaries about the league and was thinking about making a feature film.

Indeed, Marshall's 1992 film, *A League of Their Own,*

introduced the All-American Girls Professional Baseball League to more people than had ever seen its games. With a budget of $45 to $50 million, the movie cost more to make than the league had cost to operate during its entire 12-year history. Among its other achievements, *League* gave Julie Croteau the chance to become an All-American, or at least to play one. When she heard about the movie, Croteau wrote to director Marshall to see if she could be part of the project. She didn't want to miss the chance to tell the world about something that was so close to her heart. Marshall hired her as an extra and a stunt double for actress Anne Elizabeth Ramsay.

◆ Team photo of the 1943 Rockford Peaches, as seen in Penny Marshall's film *A League of Their Own. Copyright © 1992 Columbia Pictures Industries, Inc.*

◆ *A League of Their Own* sisters Kit Keller (Lori Petty, at bat) and Dottie Hinson (Geena Davis, catching). *Copyright © 1992 Columbia Pictures Industries, Inc.*

◆ Lavonne "Pepper" Paire Davis at the 1991 reunion in Clearwater Beach, Florida. Davis's hat is a souvenir from her stint as technical adviser on the Penny Marshall film. *Photo by Sue Macy*

It's not surprising that Hollywood chose to immortalize the AAGPBL. The league was a unique experiment in American history, and four decades after it folded, people looked at its players with a mixture of curiosity and awe. Although women have gained fame in golf, tennis, figure skating, and other individual sports, they have rarely had the chance to compete as teammates, especially at the professional level. "We were pioneers, you know," said Lib Mahon. "I didn't realize it then, but we were. And every one of us values the opportunities we had, more so now than when we were playing."

If the players value their experiences, so too do the girls and women who watch baseball today and wonder why only men play the national pastime. The story of AAGPBL shows that baseball once belonged to women, too. In the 1940s and '50s, women dug in and worked together as Chicks, Belles, Peaches, and Daisies, looking to each other for support and growing stronger for it. They hit home runs, pitched shutouts, snagged grounders, and kicked dirt at umpires. They also rode buses through the night, nursed bruises and sore muscles, and played for four months straight with hardly a day off. All in all, it was a wonderful way for a woman to spend a summer. Maybe one day, it can be again.

Afterword
New Beginnings

On a muggy evening in August 1994, I sat behind first base in a nearly empty baseball stadium, watching women shag flies and chase ground balls. It was two hours before game time, but I had arrived early on purpose. I wanted to experience this new incarnation of women's baseball by myself, without thousands of spectators around me.

When I wrote the last words of the last chapter of this book in July 1992, I didn't dare believe that women's baseball would become a reality again, certainly not so soon. But here I was, face-to-face with history. The players on the field, Julie Croteau among them, were the Colorado Silver Bullets, the first women's team to play pro baseball since the All-American Girls Professional Baseball League folded forty years before. And while their outward appearance was different from the Chicks and Peaches—instead of skirts, these women wore no-nonsense baseball pants and jerseys—I couldn't help but feel the spirit of the All-American Girls game that I had researched and written about for so long.

It seemed clear, at least, that the Silver Bullets owed their existence to the AAGPBL. The film *A League of Their Own* and the subsequent books and magazine articles about the original women's league awakened a buried desire in women and girls to claim their stake in the "national pastime." After decades of cheering as men took their turns at bat, it suddenly became acceptable for women to admit that they, too, wanted to play ball. The timing couldn't have been more appropriate. With the major league season cut short by a strike over salary levels, it fell to women to remind fans that people could still play baseball for the love of the game.

Indeed, the Silver Bullets and other aspiring women baseball players seemed motivated by the same desire as the women of the AAGPBL. "I've always wanted to play baseball," said Silver Bullets catcher Elizabeth Burnham. "It's my dream come true." But the founders of the Silver Bullets announced broader goals than P. K. Wrigley ever had for the All-American Girls league. Instead of playing in a league of their own, the Silver Bullets went up against men's semi-pro and minor league teams. "[We] want to inspire girls and women to play the game of baseball at all levels, from Little League through professional leagues," said Silver Bullets officials, "and to encourage all forms of organized baseball to accept women athletes as players."

Fittingly, the Silver Bullets turned to the women of the AAGPBL to help introduce their new team. On that muggy night in August, former Grand Rapids Chicks outfielder Lois "Tommie" Barker threw out the first ball as the Silver Bullets met the Ramapo (New Jersey) White Sox. Other AAGPBL players were similarly honored at other Silver Bullets games, but the older women withheld their unconditional support of the team. "The Silver Bullets are going to try and get women into major league baseball," said Fort Wayne Daisies pitching star Dottie Wiltse Collins. "Ninety-nine percent of us don't think that's the way to go." Instead, AAGPBL players have rallied behind efforts to bring back their own league, reworked slightly for the 1990s. When it debuts in 1995, the All-American Girls Professional Baseball League will become the All-American *Women*'s Professional Baseball League.

While the Silver Bullets and the AAWPBL seem to be the most promising new baseball opportunities for women, they're not the only ones. In 1994, promoters also announced plans for two other women's baseball leagues, as well as a women's professional fast-pitch softball league. And women continued to try to break into organized baseball on an individual basis. On February 15, 1994, Southern California College left-hander Ila Borders made history as the first woman to pitch for a men's college team. In that outing, Borders notched a five-hit complete game victory. She went 2–4 for the season with a 2.92 E.R.A.

It's not likely that all the new efforts in women's baseball will succeed, but whatever the future of baseball, women will be a part of it. As they should be. After all, playing baseball was a wonderful way for a woman to spend a summer in the 1940s and '50s. It will be no less wonderful as the twentieth century ends and a new one begins.

Sue Macy
October 1994

Appendix

AAGPBL RULES AND EQUIPMENT CHANGES

Year	Circumference of Ball	Length of Base Paths	Pitching Distance	Pitching Style
1943	12 inches	65 feet	40 feet	Underhand
1944	11½ inches	68 feet	"	"
1945	"	"	42 feet	"
1946	11 inches	72 feet	43 feet	Underhand and Sidearm
1947	"	"	"	Sidearm Only
1948	10⅜ inches	"	50 feet	Overhand and Sidearm*
1949	10 inches	"	55 feet	"
1950	"	"	"	"
1951	"	"	"	"
1952	"	"	"	"
1953	"	75 feet	56 feet	"
1954	9 to 9¼ inches*	85 feet**	60 feet***	"

* Same as in major league baseball
** 5 feet shorter than in major league baseball
*** 6 inches shorter than in major league baseball

Source: *The Development and Decline of the All-American Girls Baseball League, 1943–1954*, by Merrie A. Fidler (Masters of Science Thesis, University of Massachusetts Department of Physical Education, September 1976), p. 110.

ALL-AMERICAN GIRLS PROFESSIONAL
BASEBALL LEAGUE TEAMS, 1943–1954

City (State) Nickname	Years
Kenosha (Wisconsin) Comets	1943–1951
Racine (Wisconsin) Belles	1943–1950*
Rockford (Illinois) Peaches	1943–1954
South Bend (Indiana) Blue Sox	1943–1954
Milwaukee (Wisconsin) Chicks	1944†
Minneapolis (Minnesota) Millerettes	1944**
Fort Wayne (Indiana) Daisies	1945–1954
Grand Rapids (Michigan) Chicks	1945–1954
Muskegon (Michigan) Lassies	1946–1950††
Peoria (Illinois) Redwings	1946–1951
Chicago (Illinois) Colleens	1948
Springfield (Illinois) Sallies	1948
Kalamazoo (Michigan) Lassies	1950–1954
Battle Creek (Michigan) Belles	1951–1952***
Muskegon (Michigan) Belles	1953

* Moved to Battle Creek, 1951
† Moved to Grand Rapids, 1945
** Became the Fort Wayne Daisies, 1945
†† Moved to Kalamazoo, June 15, 1950
*** Moved to Muskegon, 1953

CHAMPIONSHIP TEAMS, 1943–1954

Year	Pennant Winner	Play-off Winner	Manager of Play-off Winner
1943	Racine	Racine	Johnny Gottselig
1944	Milwaukee	Milwaukee	Max Carey
1945	Rockford	Rockford	Bill Allington
1946	Racine	Racine	Leo Murphy
1947	Muskegon	Racine	Johnny Rawlings
1948	Grand Rapids	Rockford	Bill Allington
1949	Rockford	Rockford	Bill Allington
1950	Rockford	Rockford	Bill Allington
1951	South Bend	South Bend	Karl Winsch
1952	Fort Wayne	South Bend	Karl Winsch
1953	Fort Wayne	Grand Rapids	Woody English
1954	Fort Wayne	Kalamazoo	Mitch Skupien

BATTING CHAMPIONS, 1943–1954 (300 or more at-bats)

Year	Player, Team	At-Bats	Average
1943	Gladys Davis, Rockford	349	.332
1944	Betsy Jochum, South Bend	433	.296
1945	Helen Callahan, Fort Wayne	408	.299
1946	Dorothy Kamenshek, Rockford	408	.316
1947	Dorothy Kamenshek, Rockford	366	.306
1948*	Audrey Wagner, Kenosha	417	.312
1949	Doris Sams, Muskegon	408	.279
1950	Betty Weaver Foss, Fort Wayne	361	.346
1951	Betty Weaver Foss, Fort Wayne	342	.368
1952	Joanne Weaver, Fort Wayne	314	.344
1953	Joanne Weaver, Fort Wayne	410	.346
1954	Joanne Weaver, Fort Wayne	333	.429

* First year overhand pitching was allowed.

PITCHING CHAMPIONS, 1943–1954
(20 or more games, based on earned run average)

Year	Player, Team	Won	Lost	E.R.A.
1943	Helen Nicol, Kenosha	31	8	1.81
1944	Helen Nicol, Kenosha	17	11	0.93
1945	Connie Wisniewski, Grand Rapids	32	11	0.81
1946	Connie Wisniewski, Grand Rapids	33	9	0.96
1947	Mildred Earp, Grand Rapids	20	8	0.68
1948*	Alice Haylett, Grand Rapids	25	5	0.77
1949	Lois Florreich, Rockford	22	7	0.67
1950	Jean Faut, South Bend	21	9	1.12
1951	Alma Ziegler, Grand Rapids	14	8	1.26
1952	Jean Faut, South Bend	20	2	0.93
1953	Jean Faut, South Bend	17	11	1.51
1954	Janet Rumsey, South Bend	15	6	2.18

* First year overhand pitching was allowed.

Chronology

1939

May 17 Princeton University beats Columbia 2–1 in the first baseball game ever televised.

August 26 Station W2XBS in New York City televises the first major league baseball games, a doubleheader between the Cincinnati Reds and the Brooklyn Dodgers.

September 1 World War II begins as German troops invade Poland.

1940

October 16 More than 16 million American men register for the first peacetime draft in U.S. history.

Also Twenty-eight percent of all American women have jobs outside the home.

1941

December 7   Japan attacks U.S. naval forces at Pearl Harbor, Hawaii.

December 8   President Franklin D. Roosevelt declares war on Japan, calling December 7, 1941, "a date which will live in infamy."

1942

May 27   The Women's Army Auxiliary Corps begins recruiting women for the Army.

September 10   The War Department announces that women will train to fly military planes within the United States. By 1945 close to 2,000 women will serve as WASPs, or Women's Airforce Service Pilots.

1943

February 17   Philip K. Wrigley issues a press release announcing his plans to start the All-American Girls Softball League.

May   Wrigley's league begins its first season, with four teams. By September, "Baseball" has replaced "Softball" in the league's name, and more than 176,000 fans have come to games.

1944

May   After spring training and charm school, the AAGPBL begins its second season with six teams.

June 6   Combined forces from the United States, Britain, and Canada invade Normandy, France, on D Day, turning the tide against Hitler's troops.

November 7	Franklin Roosevelt is elected to his fourth term as U.S. president.
Also	Thirty-six percent of all American women have jobs outside the home.

1945

April 12	Roosevelt dies. Vice President Harry S Truman is sworn in as the nation's 33rd president.
April 30	Adolf Hitler commits suicide in Berlin.
May 8	One day after Germany surrenders, Americans and Europeans celebrate V-E Day, the end of the war in Europe.
August 14	After the United States explodes two atomic bombs over Japan in less than a week, the Japanese surrender.
August 15	Americans celebrate V-J Day, for Victory in Japan.
October 23	Jackie Robinson signs a contract to join a Brooklyn Dodgers' farm team, the Montreal Royals, for the 1946 season.

1946

March 5	Former British prime minister Winston Churchill warns that an "iron curtain" has fallen between the Communist and democratic nations of Europe.
May	The AAGPBL begins its fourth season, with eight teams. By the end of the summer, more than 750,000 people will attend league games.

Also   Thirty-one percent of all American women
                  have jobs outside the home.

1947

April 15   Jackie Robinson plays his first game for the
                  Brooklyn Dodgers, becoming the first
                  African-American to play in the major
                  leagues in the twentieth century.

July 5   Larry Doby signs with the Cleveland Indians,
                  becoming the first African-American player
                  in the American League.

September 30   The New York Yankees meet the Brooklyn
                  Dodgers in the first World Series game shown
                  on TV.

1948

May   The AAGPBL begins its peak year with 10
                  teams. By the end of the season, more than
                  910,000 fans will pay to see league games.

November 2   Truman is elected president over New York
                  governor Thomas E. Dewey.

Also   Thirty-one women win a settlement of
                  $55,000 from the Chrysler Corporation,
                  which had laid them off to hire male war
                  veterans.

1949

May   The AAGPBL begins its seventh season, with
                  eight regular teams and two rookie touring
                  teams.

September 23   Truman reports to Americans that the Soviet
                  Union has built and tested its own atomic
                  bomb.

October 1	Chinese leader Mao Tse-tung declares that mainland China is Communist.
Also	Thirty-three percent of American women have jobs outside the home, the result of a slow but steady increase since 1946.

1950

January 31	Truman announces that the United States is developing a hydrogen bomb hundreds of times more powerful than the atomic bombs dropped over Japan.
February 9	Senator Joseph McCarthy of Wisconsin sets off an anti-Communist furor when he charges that the U.S. State Department is full of Communists.
February 15	American sportswriters vote Mildred "Babe" Didrikson Zaharias the greatest female athlete of the half-century.
June 25	War breaks out in Korea when 75,000 Communist forces from the north invade South Korea.

1951

June 14	The Census Bureau in Philadelphia begins using Univac 1, the first commercially built computer.
August 11	WCBS-TV televises the first baseball games in color as the Brooklyn Dodgers meet the Boston Braves for a doubleheader in Brooklyn.
Also	Disk jockey Alan Freed coins the term *rock 'n' roll*.

1952

May — After the Peoria Redwings and Kenosha Comets fold, the AAGPBL starts its tenth season with only six teams.

November 1 — The United States tests its first hydrogen bomb.

November 4 — General Dwight D. Eisenhower is elected president. Richard Nixon is his vice president.

1953

April 3 — The first issue of *TV Guide* is published. Within a year, the magazine's circulation will be 1,500,000.

June 19 — Americans Julius and Ethel Rosenberg are executed for selling atomic bomb secrets to the Soviet Union. The Rosenbergs maintain their innocence to the end.

July 27 — After three years, the fighting in Korea is over.

Also — Sixty percent of American homes now have TV sets.

1954

May 17 — In *Brown v. Board of Education of Topeka*, the U.S. Supreme Court rules that racial segregation in public schools is illegal.

July 6 — Nineteen-year-old Elvis Presley cuts his first record.

August 12 — *Sports Illustrated* publishes its first issue. By the end of the year, its circulation will be 600,000.

September   After a season characterized by low attendance, all five remaining AAGPBL teams
fold.

Also   Thirty-five percent of American women hold
jobs outside the home. Americans buy their
first TV dinners; for 99 cents, diners get tur-
key with all the trimmings.

RECLAIMING THE PAST
1980–1993

1980
October   AAGPBL player-turned-printer June Peppas
writes and publishes the first AAGPBL newsletter.

1981
September   A letter by Fran Janssen, asking all former
players to write to Peppas, appears in
Women's Sports magazine.

1982
July 8   Some 200 former players meet in Chicago for
the league's first national reunion.

1983
September 24   Players compete in the first annual AAGPBL
old-timers game in Fort Wayne, Indiana.

1987
September 19   The AAGPBL Players Association holds its
first official meeting.

Also   Two documentaries about the AAGPBL are
                   shown on public television.

1988

November 4   The National Baseball Hall of Fame in Coo-
                   perstown, N.Y., opens its permanent
                   "Women in Baseball" exhibit.

1992

July 1   Penny Marshall's film about the AAGPBL, *A
                   League of Their Own*, opens across the
                   United States.

September 15   By this date, *A League of Their Own* has
                   grossed more than $100 million dollars,
                   making it one of the hit movies of the sum-
                   mer.

1993

August 4   The players hold a reunion in South Bend,
                   Indiana, to commemorate the 50th anniver-
                   sary of the founding of the AAGPBL.

Notes on Sources

I first became aware of the All-American Girls Professional Baseball League in the spring of 1981, when I found a two-page write-up on it in *First of All: Significant "Firsts" by American Women,* by Joan McCullough (Holt, Rinehart and Winston, New York, 1980). I was curious enough to look for more information, but when I searched other books on sports and women's history, I found virtually nothing on the league. Magazines proved a bit more helpful. The April 1976 issue of *womenSports* included an article by W. G. Nicholson chronicling the history of the AAGPBL. *Colliers, McCall's, Holiday,* and other popular magazines of the 1940s and '50s offered close to 20 features on the league and its players.

These articles gave me solid background from which to do further research. Fran Janssen's September 1981 letter to the editor of *Women's Sports* (formerly *womenSports*) helped to provide a context for that research. Janssen's letter called for former All-Americans to get in touch with June Peppas, who had just started publishing a newsletter to bring the women up-to-date on each other's lives. I contacted Janssen and Peppas and was able to obtain a mailing list of all the players they had located.

Through Peppas, I also learned that Merrie Fidler, a high school English teacher in California, had written an unpublished masters thesis on the league. I wrote to Fidler, who graciously sent me a copy of her work, *The Development and Decline of the All-American Girls Baseball League, 1943–1954*. This manuscript is an excellent study of the organizational history of the AAGPBL. In the course of her research, Fidler corresponded with Philip K. Wrigley, interviewed Arthur Meyerhoff, and pored through many of the league's administrative records. Her work was an important reference in writing this book.

In January 1982, I mailed a four-page survey to 218 former players and chaperones. The survey solicited information on how the women first heard about the league, what they liked most and least about being All-Americans, how they interacted with fans, what they did after leaving the AAGPBL, and other related issues. By April 1982, I had received responses from 105 women. The majority of the players had not reflected publicly about their baseball days for decades, and they were very generous with their replies. Many elaborated on their answers with letters that included vivid descriptions of their favorite fans or their most memorable games. Some sent photographs, newspaper clippings, and pages from their scrapbooks.

Besides my survey and Fidler's thesis, much of the material in this book was gathered from personal interviews that I conducted with players in 1982, 1983, 1985, and 1991. I did a number of these at league reunions and supplemented them with longer interviews done during trips to Pennsylvania, Texas, California, Michigan, and Indiana. I also made extensive use of the newspaper clippings, scorecards, yearbooks, and letters saved in scrapbooks by individual players, especially Ruth Williams Heverly, Fran Janssen, Ruth Lessing,

◆ Cooperstown, 1988—Author Sue Macy with ex-players Kay Heim McDaniel and Rose Gacioch. *Courtesy of Kay Heim McDaniel*

and Irene Hickson. And I spent several days using the All-American Girls Professional Baseball League Collection at the Northern Indiana Historical Society (NIHS) in South Bend. The NIHS, which houses the official AAGPBL archives, is an excellent source of material, including the scrapbooks of pitcher Dottie Wiltse Collins and a catalog of more than 1,000 photographs.

For statistical material on the league, I depended on four main sources: Fidler's thesis; the year-end batting and pitching records compiled by the Howe News Bureau in Chicago; statistical summaries in team yearbooks; and the four series of AAGBL baseball cards published in the 1980s and early '90s by historian Sharon Roepke. The cards, created with the cooperation of the league's Players' Association, present statistical and biographical data on more than 80 players.

In the course of my research, I read newspaper accounts of hundreds of league games. Despite the sometimes subjective descriptions of the players and their accomplishments, these articles went a long way toward helping me imagine the excitement surrounding the AAGPBL. During the summer months, the papers in league cities generally ran at least one article on their home team every day. Among the newspapers whose coverage I researched thoroughly were the *South Bend Tribune,* the *Grand Rapids Herald,* and *Grand Rapids Press,* the *Racine Journal-Times,* and the *Kalamazoo Gazette.*

For More About the AAGPBL

When Penny Marshall's movie *A League of Their Own* was released in July 1992, it generated a flood of articles on the AAGPBL. The film's premiere also was accompanied by the publication of the first book about the league, *Girls of Summer,* by Lois Browne (HarperCollins Publishers, New York, 1992).

Marshall's movie takes a fictionalized look at the first year the women's league was in operation. Two documentary films made in 1987 include actual footage of AAGPBL games and interviews with former stars. *When Diamonds Were a Girl's Best Friend* was produced and directed by Janis L. Taylor. *A League of Their Own,* the documentary that inspired Marshall's movie, was produced by Kim Wilson and Kelly Candaele.

Local history museums in some league towns have collections of material on their teams and occasionally offer exhibits. The Northern Indiana Historical Society (NIHS) periodically exhibits memorabilia from the league. For information on museum hours or access to the AAGPBL archives there, write to the NIHS at 808 West Washington, South Bend, Indiana 46601, or call (219) 235-9664.

The National Baseball Hall of Fame and Museum in Cooperstown, New York, has a permanent "Women in Baseball" exhibit, and more than half of it is devoted to the AAGPBL. The museum is open seven days a week, closed only on Thanksgiving, Christmas, and New Year's Day. For museum hours call (607) 547-9988. The Hall of Fame's library has a small collection of photographs and printed material on the league.

Anyone interested in league-related news and activities can join the AAGPBL Players' Association for an annual fee. For more information, write to the AAGPBL Players' Association, Inc., c/o Dottie Collins, 1929 Jessie Avenue, Fort Wayne, Indiana 46808.

For information on AAGBL baseball cards, contact Sharon Roepke, P.O. Box 3332, Kalamazoo, Michigan 49003-3332.

For Further Reading

On Major League Baseball
in the 1940s

Gilbert, Bill. *They Also Served: Baseball and the Home Front, 1941–1945.* New York: Crown Publishers, Inc., 1992. Gilbert deals mostly with the major leagues. He includes only a paragraph about the AAGPBL.

Halberstam, David. *Summer of '49.* New York: William Morrow and Company, Inc., 1989. This is a terrific book about the rivalry between the New York Yankees and the Boston Red Sox after the war. It captures the excitement and flavor of major league baseball in the late forties.

Peterson, Robert. *Only the Ball Was White: A History of Legendary Black Players and All-Black Professional Teams.* Old Tappan, N.J.: Prentice-Hall, 1970. Reissued by Oxford University Press, 1992. Peterson gives an overview of the players and teams of the Negro leagues. He includes a brief mention of female player Toni Stone.

On Life in the United States
During and After the War

Bailey, Ronald H., and the Editors of Time-Life Books. *World War II: The Home Front: U.S.A.* Alexandria, Va.: Time-Life Books Inc., 1978.

This cultural and pictorial history paints a compelling picture of life on the homefront, although it doesn't include the AAGPBL.

Dickson, Paul. *Timelines: Day by Day and Trend by Trend from the Dawn of the Atomic Age to the Close of the Cold War*. Reading, Mass.: Addison-Wesley Publishing Company, Inc., 1990. Dickson presents an easy-to-use chronicle of cultural, social, and political events from 1945 to 1989.

On Women During and After the War

Gluck, Sherna Berger. *Rosie the Riveter Revisited: Women, the War, and Social Change*. Boston: Twayne Publishers, 1987. Gluck spent several years interviewing more than 200 women war workers. This book includes oral histories and commentary.

Harris, Mark Jonathan; Mitchell, Franklin D.; and Schechter, Steven J. *The Homefront: America During World War II*. New York: G. P. Putnam's Sons, 1984. The authors compiled oral histories about the war from men and women and arranged them in thematic chapters, including one on Rosie the Riveter.

Keil, Sally Van Wagenen. *Those Wonderful Women in Their Flying Machines: The Unknown Heroines of World War II*. New York: Rawson, Wade Publishers, Inc., 1979. Keil takes a fascinating, detailed look at another World War II phenomenon, the Women's Airforce Service Pilots (WASPs).

May, Elaine Tyler. *Homeward Bound: American Families in the Cold War*. New York: Basic Books, 1988. Although written for an academic audience, this book contains an interesting analysis of the renewed emphasis on the family after World War II.

Nelson, Mariah Burton. *Are We Winning Yet? How Women Are Changing Sports and Sports Are Changing Women*. New York: Random House, 1991. Nelson looks at some outstanding women athletes, including baseball player Julie Croteau, as she explores the relationship between women and the sports they play.

Weatherford, Doris. *American Women and World War II*. New York: Facts on File, Inc., 1990. Written for young adults, this is a thorough account of women in the military and on the homefront during the war. Weatherford does not mention the AAGPBL.

Index

umpires, 11, 47, *48*, 78–80, 83, 109
  women as, xvii
uniforms, 12, 72, 95–96
United Nations, *91*
United Press, 14

Varga, 39
Voyce, Inez, 47

Wagner, Audrey, *55–56, 60,* 101
Ward, Gadget, *48*
war effort, *3,* 4, 36–37. *See also* homefront.
Weaver, Joanne, 49, *56, 61,* 98
Wegman, Marie "Blackie," 72
Wenzel, Marge, *38*
Whiting, Betty, 47
Williams, Ruth, 25, 26, 29, 56, 68, 79
Williams, Ted, 22
William Wrigley Jr. chewing-gum company, 4
Wills, Helen, 7
Winsch, Karl, 20, 56
Winter, Joanne, 35, 42–43, 44, 49, *50,* 101
Wirth, Senaida "Shoo Shoo," 74
Wisniewski, Connie, 49, *58*
women, as athletes
  growing fame in 1930s of, 7
  Philip K. Wrigley and, 14–15
  more recent strategies of, 20
  AAGPBL and, 41
  effect on later lives of, 102–103
  fame of, 108
women, as baseball players, 108–109
  Philip K. Wrigley and, xvi, 6, 8
  prevailing attitudes toward, 22

childhood encouragement of, 22–25, 30–31
  AAGPBL's development of, 49–51
  African-Americans and, 53
  community of, 64–65
  press's attitude toward, 84
  rarity of, 98
  NCAA and, 99
  historical neglect of, 104–105
  See also "femininity" and the AAGPBL.
women, as major league owners, xvii
women, as managers, 26
women, as umpires, xvii
"Women in Baseball" display, *xvii,* xvii–xviii, 105
women, in National Baseball Hall of Fame, xv, *xvii*–xviii, 105
women, in work force, 2, 4, *5,* 92–93, 100, 101
women, married, 2, 65, 92, 93, 94–95, 100–101
Women's Army Corps (WAC), 35
Women's Professional Basketball League (WBL), 20
women's role in society
  World War II and, xviii, 2
  Philip K. Wrigley and, 14–15
  postwar era and, 92–93, 103
  AAGPBL in conflict with, 98
  1970s and '80s and, 105
Women's Tennis Association (WTA), 20
World Series, *91*
World War II, xvi, xviii, 1, 2, *5,* 33, 35, 37, 40–41, 44, 66, 90, 92, 95, 100
Wrigley Field, 8, 35–36
Wrigley, Helen, 12